"I really enjoyed the st(
that I cried… It had intr
the way it allowed diffe

~Cheryl Chapman ,--

"This book led to the most lively discussions our group had during its two years together. Everybody had an opinion, and this material generated passionate reactions. Every care group leader dreads those evenings when no one says anything—that will not be a concern with this book! We would recommend this study to any care group that is prepared to get serious about what Scripture has to say about money. Just be prepared for a little bit of controversy!"

~Glen and Christie Hoos (Abbotsford, BC)
Small Group Leaders & Power to Change* Missionaries
(*formerly Campus Crusade for Christ)

"This book tackles a challenging and very important issue in a humorous, engaging, and thoughtful way. As I led a small group through this study, it revealed a wide range of attitudes towards wealth, poverty, and giving. We need teaching like this about wealth: balanced and lighthearted enough that it wins you over, and so solidly Biblical that it's hard to walk away from."

~Tim Hardy (Victoria, BC)
Small Group Leader (mixed group)

"Your Money Or Your Life is an intelligent yet easy to read book. It is written with a gentle spirit and in a thoughtful, non-judgmental manner. Our small group, like the characters, was challenged to develop Christlike responses to our earthly possessions.

"The book has a very strong scriptural foundation from which financial principles and concepts are drawn and applied to our lives. Discussions revealed how group members felt both challenged and affirmed with how they use their financial resources for the benefit of their neighbours and the growth of the Kingdom. The study is relevant to a society that tends toward excess."

~Ian & Shari Watson (Calgary, AB)
Leaders of a group of couples with young children

Your Money
or **Your Life**

Your Money
or Your Life

Can You Do Both God's Way?

Russell Corben
with Brian Smith

YOUR MONEY OR YOUR LIFE
Can You Do Both God's Way?

by Russell Corben with Brian Smith

Copyright © 2007 Russell Corben

ISBN # 1-897373-15-5

Published by Word Alive Inc.

131 Cordite Road, Winnipeg, Manitoba, R3W 1S1
www.wordalive.ca

Table of Contents

Supplemental Studies:

AN UNUSUAL PROLOGUE

REVEREND MOSS'S SERMON that Sunday morning had barely started. The topic was joyful generosity, and my mind soon drifted back to my warm bed. I may even have dozed off momentarily. But my tranquility was rudely shattered by a loud bellow from behind.

"I can't believe you're talking about money again! Enough guilt already! You're making people angry and turning them off!"

My head whipped around, along with four hundred others, to see a red-faced man in the last pew gesturing wildly toward the pulpit. It was Brian—a gruff, intimidating sort, but I must say I never suspected that he would stand up during a service and start shouting. A few folks near the sermon-stopper half-rose and reached toward him, perhaps attempting to pull him back down into his seat. Or maybe they wanted to lay hands on him and pray for exorcism?

I exchanged a wide-eyed glance with my girlfriend, Jennifer, sitting beside me. No one in our church had ever interrupted a speaker before. If people disagreed with an authority figure, they expressed themselves in the time-

1

honoured Christian way—they complained behind closed doors to like-minded allies.

But Brian's outburst did not ruffle the Reverend Harold Moss. With calm authority, he replied, "I was wondering if anyone was listening. Thank you, Brian, for your...concern." He gave the congregation a little smile and nodded toward the disrupter. "The Bible's radical teachings about money, riches, and giving are challenging for all of us. Or rather, they're challenging for those who listen." I was sure I saw Reverend Moss's eyes flicker in my direction. I shrank down in my seat.

Jennifer nudged my arm and, with a smirk, whispered, "Were you sleeping, Joe?"

Instead of answering, I turned pointedly toward Brian, just in time to see him re-seat himself and cross his arms stubbornly, muttering under his breath.

After a pause, our minister once again addressed the congregation. "Sometimes in guilt, worry, confusion, or fear, we turn away from topics relating to money. But anyone who believes and obeys the Bible will discover a treasure trove of joy and wisdom in its many passages about money and possessions, and giving and sharing. In fact, in two weeks, one of our adult Sunday school classes will offer an eleven-week study on money and giving. I encourage you to attend.

"We are aliens and strangers in this world, and we find greatest fulfillment when we use our wealth with a view toward our true, eternal home. That's why God wants us to be joyfully generous. Which brings us back to our sermon topic today. Please open your Bibles to...."

A Sneak Peak Ahead

That's how it started.

In just a moment, we'll return to my story with Jennifer, Reverend Moss, and several other characters—both ordinary and amazing. But first, let me give you some idea of what to expect.

You are about to join me in a series of eleven innovative Bible studies on money, possessions, and—at the center of our focus—generosity. The lessons are suitable for small group discussion or for individual study, and each will examine at least one key Bible passage in depth.

These studies are based on my experience in an adult Sunday school class on "Joyful Generosity." Join me and my six fellow class members—including Bill, our wise and gentle leader—as the group discusses and debates several of the most important and best-known Bible passages on money, possessions, and giving.

But be warned—this is not just a journey for the mind, but for the heart as well. The experience changed every member of the class in some way, and the process wasn't always pleasant. If you come with us, prepare to wrestle with the same challenges we faced week after week.

Scattered throughout each chapter's narrative are questions intended for private and group study, discussion, and life application. You may want to keep a separate notebook in which to write your responses to these questions. You'll also find a few extra notes on Bible background and language that relate to the passages.

I've ended each chapter with a Brief Debrief, which highlights the most important points our group learned that week. The Debrief also contains a few concluding questions to help you decide what practical steps to take as you seek to live out what God is teaching you.

If you're using this book in a group, I suggest that each member read the week's chapter in advance and take a little time to ponder the questions—especially the ones that guide you in self-examination and life application. Or your group could read the chapter aloud at the beginning of your time together. In any case, our group found it helpful to read each week's Bible passage twice before studying it.

Details came up on the second reading that we hadn't noticed the first time around.

At the end of the book, I've also included a few "Supplemental Studies" that deal with other fascinating passages that our group didn't have time to study together.

Now let me take you back to that opening week when the "Joyful Generosity" class met for the first time. As I tell the story of that initial meeting, I'll offer a few questions that your small group might want to discuss during your introductory meeting.

Here we go…

Conflicting Agendas at the Doorway to Joy

IT WAS ALL MY GIRLFRIEND'S FAULT. She insisted that we both needed to learn more about money in the Bible. And when Jennifer insists, you listen.

So, two weeks after Brian's big scene, I found myself sitting in an adult Sunday school room in a circle of chairs with four other people—three of whom I knew slightly. Beside me was Cathy, a woman in her thirties whose tummy partially filled a pastel maternity dress. Across the circle sat Sue Coyne, a thin, elderly widow and long-time church member. A young woman who looked to be in her mid-twenties sat beside Mrs. Coyne, talking with her quietly. And I was most surprised to see Wayman, a short, unpleasant man who only occasionally attended church.

The door opened, and in walked my girlfriend, Jennifer, assisting a bright-eyed, elderly man who walked slowly with a cane. Once again, I found myself enchanted by Jennifer's blonde hair and beautiful, smiling blue eyes as she and the gentleman made their way to two of the empty chairs.

Once they were settled, Jennifer announced pleasantly, "Welcome, everyone. My name is Jennifer, and I'm the church administrator. I was asked to introduce our leader, Bill." She gestured to the man beside her. "Bill started attending this church just a couple of months ago. He ran a bakery for a long time here in the city, and I've made him promise to bring in some baked goodies on occasion." A few people chuckled.

What's so funny? I wondered. Food is serious business!

Our teacher, who appeared to be about seventy—maybe older—had a shock of disordered white hair and wore a rumpled cardigan sweater. In spite of his apparent infirmity, when Bill leaned forward and spoke, it was with surprising energy.

"I apologize for being late," he said. "I don't move as quickly as I used to. My son says it's because I'm getting old. But the real reason is that I was born at such an early age."

Wayman snickered.

"Why don't we start with introductions? Tell us your name and what keeps you busy during the week. Then give one reason why you've come to this class. What do you want to learn? Jennifer, do you mind starting?"

My girlfriend gave a quick nod. "All right. Besides working part-time here at the church, I've almost completed a master's degree in business. My reason for coming…" She thought for a moment. "I want to be a good steward of what God has given me. So, I'd like to learn how to avoid the dangers of debt—particularly credit card debt." She glanced my way and frowned before I could extinguish my knowing grin. I liked to tease her about being a shopaholic. Yet, at the same time, Jennifer always put the required amount in the church offering.

How does she do it? I asked myself. *She's no better off than I am.* As much as I wanted to be a faithful steward, I rarely succeeded at giving ten percent. *Maybe if I tithe on my take-home pay instead of my gross income, I could swing it... I wonder if Bill will talk about that?*

I emerged from my reverie to realize that all eyes were focused on me. "Oh, uh, I'm Joe." Then I regained my poise. "I'm a high school gym teacher. I want to learn about saving wisely for retirement. Other teachers tell me that our mandatory pension plan won't be enough, but I have trouble saving on my own. So I'm curious about how all that fits into a Christian's thinking about money."

Cathy was next. "I'm a mother of two young daughters, with one more child on the way." She patted her slightly rounded stomach. "My husband, Bob, is an engineer. I'm also a part-time sales rep for a cosmetics company, working out of our apartment.

"We're hoping to buy a house for our growing family, but it's difficult. Raising a family is such a heavy financial responsibility. I don't know how much we'll be able to give when we have to make mortgage payments."

When Cathy finished, the group turned toward Wayman, a small man with a large, misshapen head and a narrow, close-trimmed beard. Wayman had always seemed slippery and dishonest to me, and I never saw him chatting with anyone before or after church. *Why is he even here?* I wondered. *I guess a class like this draws all types.*

In a loud, gruff voice, he said, "Wayman is my name. I own the Best Deal Discount Vehicle lot down on Second Avenue."

A used car dealer! It figures.

"I have three kids," Wayman continued, "and I just want to show them how to be smart with their money." Then he turned suddenly toward Mrs. Coyne.

Mrs. Coyne opened her mouth, then closed it, caught off guard by Wayman's abrupt finish. Then, in a crisp, businesslike manner, the elderly woman said, "I'm Susan Coyne. I was a housewife for almost forty years, but I lost my husband three years ago. My son and daughter are both married with their own children. They all live so far away that I seldom get to see them. But I'm delighted to say that my granddaughter just moved into town." She smiled and squeezed the hand of the young woman beside her.

She went on, "I live on a fixed income, and there's very little extra for me to play around with. However, I do want to find out what the Bible says about giving wisely." Here Mrs. Coyne began to pick up steam. "Frankly, it bothers me when street people ask me for a hand-out. I *know* most of them use it for alcohol or drugs. And while we're talking about squandering money, I've heard many stories about churches and so-called 'Christian' ministries wasting money or even stealing donations. I won't have a penny of my money going to such unworthy causes. No, sir!" She pounded her Bible with a bony fist.

Good point, I thought. In fact, I really wondered about the fancy new curtains and carpet our church bought last year. No one blinked an eye at the cost. But there sure was a big fight over the colours!

My mind returned to the group in time for the next introduction.

"My name is Samantha," the young woman beside Mrs. Coyne said to a spot on the floor. She nervously pushed back her glasses with one finger, as though they were slipping down her nose. "I'm…well, I live with my six year-old son, Cody." She glanced furtively at her grandmother, breathed deeply, then continued. "I'm a waitress at Burger Queen. I'm curious about how God wants to bless us…you know, with money and things. I saw a TV preacher last week who said he gave away his old, broken-down car and claimed a new one for his ministry. The next day there was a brand new Lexus in his driveway! He said we can all do that, but I've prayed, and it hasn't worked for me. So…"

Samantha stopped and looked over at Bill, who frowned slightly. He said, "Samantha, I think you're talking about the so-called 'Health and Wealth Gospel,' and it happens that the class will address that very issue later in the series. After all," he paused and smiled, "I'm quite familiar with material blessing, having made a lot of *bread* in my day." The pun elicited a few groans.

Our leader pretended not to hear them. "As for me, I am indeed a retired baker, as Jennifer said. I guess you could say that most people make bread from dough, but I also made dough from my bread!"

Louder groans.

"Puns are the highest form of humour, you know," said Bill with another smile. "Thank you each for introducing yourselves. I trust we'll build some good friendships. And keep in mind, the more you contribute, the more we'll all learn—including me. I love discussing the Bible with people because I always come away with something new."

Bill stopped to gather his thoughts, then continued, "Why don't we begin by establishing some working definitions for a few key words? Let's define the words 'riches' and 'wealth' as referring to monetary riches and material wealth. We can be rich in many ways, but for the purposes of this class, we'll take the word 'rich' to mean 'having a lot of money and possessions' or 'having a high standard of living.' Same thing with the word 'generous.' We can be generous with our time or abilities, but let's define 'generosity' as 'giving or sharing our money and possessions.'

What do you hope to get out of these Bible studies? What will you invest in order to reap this benefit?

"You'll also hear the word 'joy' come up a lot. I like to define biblical joy as 'a deep, enduring confidence in God,' rather than temporary happiness. Putting all of this together, then, means that Joyful Generosity, the name of our class, would be defined as the 'giving and sharing of our money and possessions because of our deep, enduring confidence in God.'

"Is it okay with everyone to start out with these working definitions?"

Most heads nodded yes. Wayman frowned and narrowed his eyes.

Bill said, "Money and giving are major topics in the Bible. In fact, Jesus talked more about money than about heaven and hell combined.

When you think about money, possessions, and giving in the Bible, which verses or stories come to mind?

Why is it important to study what the Bible says about money and possessions?

"Our aim is to follow God's model of generosity toward us by being joyfully generous ourselves. This isn't an easy goal to achieve, because it may mean changing values that we hold onto tightly. But in this class, our strong focus on God's Word will provide the guidance we need for the journey. The Bible won't always spell out a detailed answer to every question, but it provides all the basic principles to guide us toward joyful, godly decisions."

At this, Wayman burst out, "And what if we don't like what the Bible says?"

For a moment, Wayman's retort echoed off the walls. Bill scratched his jaw, calmly weighing his response. "Wayman," he finally replied, "your question may prove more perceptive than you realize. We must not enter into this study lightly. The Bible is a radical book, and its teachings sometimes fly in the face of common sense—or at least what the world considers common sense. Some of Jesus' teachings, in particular, appear careless and even bizarre. But giving that appears shockingly foolish to the world can prove to be a freeing act of worship for Christians. I would ask each of you to pray for wisdom to challenge the world's viewpoint, to combat rationalization and excuse-making.

"I guarantee that on some issues we will find as many opinions as there are bodies in this room. We won't always agree. But we need to talk openly about money, or we won't be able to help each other learn and grow in this vital area of life."

Bill paused to catch his breath, and Mrs. Coyne jumped in. "If you ask me, we don't hear enough about money in church.

What emotions do you feel when the topic of giving comes up?

Pastors are just plain chicken. Because we pay their salaries, they consider money and giving taboo topics."

"Except at the end of the year or during a building campaign," Wayman added, and everyone nodded.

"Money and giving are controversial topics, for sure," Bill agreed. "However, if we want to do things God's way, then we will make the Bible the source of our beliefs and actions, and the result will be unbelievable joy, both here and in eternity."

Bill checked his notes. "Speaking of the Bible, please listen or read along as I read my favourite Scripture passage—Matthew 6:19-21. I see that most of you have the New International Version, which is the translation I like to use. But feel free to bring other translations to our meetings.

"After I've read this passage, I'll ask you each to answer just one question: What does Jesus mean by his statement in verse 21—the last verse in today's passage?"

Retrieving a pair of reading glasses from his shirt pocket, Bill proceeded:

[19]Do not store up for yourselves treasures on earth, where moth and rust destroy, and where thieves break in and steal. [20]But store up for yourselves treasures in heaven, where moth and rust do not de-

**stroy, and where thieves do not break in
and steal. ²¹For where your treasure is,
there your heart will be also.**

Bill read the passage a second time and then looked up at
us. "So, what did Jesus mean, 'Where your treasure is,
there your heart will be also'?"

Mrs. Coyne charged ahead. "I think he's talking to all
those snobby, money-grabbing shysters who pass themselves off as spiritual leaders—like the Pharisees!"

"What do you mean, 'money-grabbing'?" blurted
Wayman loudly. "Jesus says nothing here against making
money. He just says to keep part of your heart for Him, for
heaven. Right?" He crossed his arms and turned to Bill.

Mrs. Coyne raised a skinny finger and was about to
launch a rejoinder in Wayman's direction when Bill extended both hands like a referee separating two boxers.
"Hold on right there," he declared. "I'm sure each of you
could make a good case for your opinions, and I believe
there's truth in what you've each said, but let's not get hos-
tile. We'll have plenty of time in future sessions to go into
greater depth on these issues."

Bill leaned back in his chair and winced slightly. "Who
would like to share next?"

Jennifer sat up straight and replied, "I think Jesus was
saying that if we handle our money exactly the way the Bible tells us to—and it's very specific on these issues—then
our hearts will be right before God and He'll be pleased
with us."

Seeing my opportunity, I jumped in as well. "That's
what I think too. Jennifer's exactly right."

Bill raised an eyebrow at me. "O-kaaay." He drew the
word out. "Thank you both. Joe, I reserve the right to have
you expand on your answer at a later date." His eyes twinkled as he held my suddenly nervous gaze for a moment
longer.

Cathy stirred in her seat, rescuing me by saying, "I can't help thinking of my girls...how each one has a special, favourite toy. It's almost as though each little heart is attached by a string to her toy. Instead, I want them to develop cords tying their hearts to the Lord and to eternal riches." Then she said quietly, "And I need that same faith myself."

Across from her, Samantha nodded slowly and said in a quiet voice, "Yeah, it's like our heart follows our treasure...what's important to us." Samantha glanced at her grandmother, who touched her hand and smiled reassuringly.

Jennifer said, "But our hearts must be in the right place before we can do anything else, Samantha."

Cathy intervened. "I don't think that's what this verse says, though, Jennifer. The placement of our treasure comes first: For where your treasure is, there your heart will be also. If we put our treasure in heaven with God, that's where our hearts will be as well."

Bill was beaming. "Thanks to each of you for sharing. This group is already on the way to a deeper understanding of God's Word." With growing excitement, he continued, "Here's the bottom line: If we trust in the Lord and His Word for guidance, we will experience great joy here on earth, and in heaven we'll receive treasure beyond what we can imagine!"

Which, if any, of the group members' summaries do you think is closest to what Jesus meant in Matthew 6:21?

For a moment, Bill was silent, lost in the picture he had just painted.

"Uh, Bill?" Jennifer held out a stack of photocopied papers. "The schedule?"

"Oh, yes, thanks for reminding me." Bill blinked several times. "Jennifer copied a list of the main passages we'll be studying each week."

Jennifer efficiently distributed the schedule* while Bill continued. "Next week we'll study the rich young ruler in Luke 18. Please try to read the passage during the week to get your mental and spiritual juices flowing.

"If there's nothing else," he concluded, "we'll see you all next week." He punctuated his last word with a thump of his cane on the floor.

The rich young ruler? I wondered. *That's a strange passage to start with. Didn't Jesus tell the ruler to sell all he had and give the money to the poor? Bill warned us that the Bible is radical, but I'm not sure I'm ready for him to preach that at me right out of the blocks.*

I followed Jennifer out of the room, uncertain whether I really wanted to come back.

A Brief Debrief

At the time, I had no idea how wise Bill's simple teaching was in our first class. But as I look back now, two principles stand out as most important:

- It's only by means of honest Scripture study and open discussion that we grow in the stewardship of the wealth God has given us.

- Godly stewardship promises great joy in this life and in the next.

If you're like I was, you probably have serious reservations about this study. That's completely natural, and I understand. But I encourage you to hang in there to see the group members grow and learn from God's Word. Give God a chance to prove Himself, because He is trustworthy. God

---

* The group's schedule is reflected in this book's table of contents.

wants what's best for us. Let God make good on His promise of joy as you come to know, above all else, the generous heart of God, the Greatest Giver.

Briefly summarize your outlook on money, possessions, and giving. How closely do you expect your outlook to align with the Bible's teaching?

Do you have an accountability partner assisting you with money management (spending, giving, etc.)? If not, would this be helpful for you?

Note to Group Leaders

In addition to discussing the questions scattered throughout this chapter, I encourage your group—especially if the members are new to each other—to spend a good part of your first meeting getting personally acquainted. It's also wise, during the first session or two, to discuss some of the expectations and ground rules for your meetings. At the end of each study, remind everyone to read the next chapter before the following meeting.

The Rich Young Man (or Woman)

I CAME BACK. Mainly because Jennifer shamed me into it. I can still hear her nagging, *You have to finish what you start.* She must have said that a dozen times in seven days.

So, I must confess that my heart was not brimming with cheer when Bill started this week's session.

"In today's Bible passage," Bill began, "Jesus confronts a man with a challenge that we may find disturbing. We'd better prepare our hearts. Joe, could you pray for us?"

I shrugged. "I can do that."

After I prayed, Bill said, "Jennifer, would you mind reading Luke 18:18-30?"

My girlfriend nodded. As we all turned to the passage, Bill suggested, "As we read, let's put ourselves into this scene. Imagine yourself there."

Then Jennifer read:

[18]A certain ruler asked him, "Good teacher, what must I do to inherit eternal life?" [19]"Why do you call me good?" Jesus answered. "No one is good—except God alone. [20]You know the commandments: 'Do not commit adultery, do not murder, do not steal, do not give false testimony, honor your father and mother.'" [21]"All these I have kept since I was a boy," he said.

[22]When Jesus heard this, he said to him, "You still lack one thing. Sell everything you have and give to the poor, and you will have treasure in heaven. Then come, follow me."

[23]When he heard this, he became very sad, because he was a man of great wealth. [24]Jesus looked at him and said, "How hard it is for the rich to enter the kingdom of God! [25]Indeed, it is easier for a camel to go through the eye of a needle than for a rich man to enter the kingdom of God."

[26]Those who heard this asked, "Who then can be saved?"

[27]Jesus replied, "What is impossible with men is possible with God."

[28]Peter said to him, "We have left all we had to follow you!"

[29]"I tell you the truth," Jesus said to them, "no one who has left home or wife or brothers or parents or children for the sake of the kingdom of God [30]will fail to receive many times as much in this age and, in the age to come, eternal life."

"One of my Sunday school teachers taught us to read a passage twice before discussing it," Bill told us. "Cathy, could you do the honours?"

That's a bit pointless, I thought at first. But as Cathy reread the passage, I must admit that I began to see details I hadn't caught the first time.

After Cathy had finished, Bill said, "Since Luke emphasizes this man's wealth, our first question today is, 'What is your definition of a wealthy person?'"

You don't have to look far to find a rich man, I thought as I glanced over at Wayman. His

FYI*: Matthew 19:16-30 and Mark 10:17-31 are parallel accounts of this story. Each account adds a few details to the story. For example, Matthew tells us that the ruler was young.*

gold watch and large ring glinted back at me. Of course, I wasn't about to say anything out loud about his wealth.

Finally, Cathy ventured a response. "A neighbour couple in our apartment building comes to mind—well, *ex*-neighbours, actually. They just bought an expensive house out in that new Highland Hills subdivision. They both have high-paying jobs and can afford many luxuries, so I'd call them rich."

Mrs. Coyne weighed in. "I think you're rich if you have more money than you know what to do with. You hear about celebrities and big company executives buying ridiculously expensive items, often to impress other people. It makes me ill to think of the waste!"

Or could it be jealousy? I wanted to ask.

"Bill," asked Cathy, looking through the window into the parking lot, "do you want us to define *rich* just for our culture or for people globally? I don't consider myself rich, but last year my husband and I went on a missions trip to Central America. Compared to those people, I'm definitely wealthy."

A smile spread across Bill's face. "The vast majority of our ancestors and people living in our world today would look at you and me as if we'd won a major lottery. When we think of everything available to us in our society, probably everyone in this room is rich."

Wayman gave Bill a threatening look. "Of course, you and I are rich if you compare us to people in India or to ancient Egyptian slaves building the pyramids. But I don't think it does any good to compare."

"I agree," Bill responded. Wayman's glare turned into a look of surprise. Bill went on, "Such comparisons can result in sinful pride or paralyzing guilt, neither of which is pleasing to God. But who doesn't ever compare himself to his neighbour? In my experience, our definition of *rich* has little to do with our level of wealth. Instead, we generally consider people rich if they have more than we do, no matter how much we have."

I realized with a start that he was right. When I was a starving college student, I thought anyone who ate in fancy restaurants and owned a respectable car was rich. Now I have a decent-paying job and a three-year-old vehicle, and I still don't feel wealthy. How much would it take to make me feel rich? I glanced at Wayman again—at his jewellery, expensive boots, and tailored suit. I wonder if he thinks he's rich?

Bill said, "I like the insight in Proverbs 30:8-9: **'Give me neither poverty nor riches, but give me only my daily bread. Otherwise, I may have too much and disown you and say, 'Who is the LORD?' Or I may become poor and steal, and so dishonor the name of my God.'"**

"That reminds me of the Lord's Prayer," I piped up. **"Give us today our daily bread."**

"So, Bill," Wayman's voice oozed sarcasm, "you're saying that if someone has more than their daily bread, they're rich?"

Bill answered, "By virtually every definition—except our own—everyone in this room is wealthy. None of us has to fear starvation. None of us is lacking the essentials of life.

We are all members of the richest society in human history."

"But I still don't feel that way," I heard Jennifer murmur.

What is your definition of a materially rich person? Do you fit this description?

Do you feel wealthy?

Bill continued, "Now, as we read, I asked everyone to imagine being there. Think about that. Through whose eyes did you see the conversation between Jesus and the rich man?"

I jumped in. "I was a member of the crowd, watching from the side."

"Me too," said Jennifer. "Although I must say I can easily see that selfish man through Jesus' eyes."

"Well," said a small, hesitant voice. We all turned to Samantha, whose hands fidgeted in her lap. "I...I was the rich ruler. And even though I knew I was self-seeking, I also saw that Jesus loved me."

Bill nodded and said, "Samantha, I think you've struck on the perspective God wants us to take. We are probably far wealthier than anyone in that crowd. Because of our wealth, then, we need to study this passage from the point of view of this rich man, not from the viewpoint of the spectators."

I noticed Jennifer stiffen.

"Perhaps rich women are off the hook, then?" Cathy suggested.

"No way!" I responded, realizing too late that she was only joking. I felt my face grow hot.

When you read the rich young ruler story, from whose viewpoint do you consider it? In what ways are you similar to and different from the rich man?

"So we're supposed to give away everything we own?" Wayman sounded downright angry now. "Sorry, but that's taking things too far!"

That's right, I thought. *Just because Jesus said that to one person in the Bible, it couldn't possibly mean that He wants all of us to do the same!*

Bill responded with a note of exasperation, "Let's be careful about putting words in people's mouths, Wayman.

No one is telling you to give everything away. However, that's exactly what every Christian must do."

Wayman's mouth gaped open. Jennifer raised her eyebrows.

That's absurd! Maybe Bill's in the early stages of Alzheimer's?

But our leader said, "When someone becomes a Christian, he gives his life to Christ. He gives up everything to God, including all money and possessions. As Peter said to Jesus, **"We have left all we had to follow you!"** All of us who are followers of Christ have made the same commitment, to devote our possessions, our money, and our very being completely to God."

Which of the rich man's assumptions did Jesus expose?

Bill allowed the room to fall silent. A couple of people nodded, while others squirmed.

Then Bill said, "Now, let's examine the rich man again. In his quest for eternal life, he asserted that he had obeyed all of God's commandments. We know now that it's impossible to truly fulfill the Old Testament Law, but at that time Jews believed it was achievable. So what happened next?"

Mrs. Coyne answered, "Jesus told that snob to sell everything he had, give to the poor, and follow Him. The man wasn't any too happy about it, either."

"In fact," interjected Jennifer, "both Matthew and Mark tell us that the rich young man walked away from Jesus. I read all three parallel accounts this week." She rolled her pretty eyes. "And what a fool, giving up eternal life for earthly wealth! He just loved his money too much."

"Yes, but…" I was hesitant to contradict Jennifer. "Maybe some of us can identify with the guy." Jennifer instantly gave me one of her plastic-sweet smiles, which I knew conveyed anything but pleasure.

It was difficult to continue with my girlfriend looking at me like that, but I stumbled ahead. "If Jesus told me to give everything away, I'd be sad inside. But outwardly, I'd act offended. After all, giving up my hard-earned wealth seems unfair. No minister, teacher, or financial planner would ever tell me to give everything away!"

Bill nodded. "Jesus' command is shocking, isn't it? It seems, though, that the man truly respected Jesus. And he knew the stakes were high. So why didn't he just obey?"

Looking down at her Bible, Cathy answered, "The passage says, '**He became very sad, because he was a man of great wealth.**' Luke assumes he loved his money because he had so much of it. He was torn between two things he couldn't have at the same time—his money and eternal life."

Mrs. Coyne raised her white eyebrows. "Isn't it obvious why he refused to obey? No rich person can obey the command to give it all away, because money always sinks its claws into the person's heart. He couldn't *help* but fall in love with it."

"It would seem, Sue," responded Bill, "that Jesus agrees with you. As the rich man walked away, Jesus said plainly, '**How hard it is for the rich to enter the kingdom of God! Indeed, it is easier for a camel to go through the eye of a needle than for a rich man to enter the kingdom of God.**'"

Bill paused to let this sink in. There were some very gloomy faces around the room. Jennifer glared at the carpet. Wayman scowled.

I spoke up, "But wasn't there an entrance to Jerusalem called the Needle's Gate? Camels had great difficulty getting through it because it was so small, like a needle's eye. Therefore, Jesus meant that it is challenging for a rich man to get into the kingdom, but not impossible."

"That idea actually turned out to be a myth, Joe," Bill answered. "There's no way around it: Jesus says it's impossible for a rich man to enter the kingdom of God."

FYI: There is no historical evidence to support the existence of a "Needle's Gate." Christ probably used this imagery because the camel was the largest animal common to Israel at the time, while the needle's eye was the smallest hole that His audience was familiar with.

After a moment, Samantha ventured, "But what about God? Can't God change even a rich person's heart?"

Bill leaned forward. "Again, I think you've hit on a key point, Samantha." He began gesturing with both hands. "Jesus went on to say, '**What is impossible with men is possible with God**.' Indeed, that is the kernel of saving grace in this self-centered world. The rich man thought his good deeds could save him, but in truth, only faith in Jesus can save us.

"But let's not ignore the danger. Being wealthy myself, I find it ominous that Jesus made a point of warning the rich so emphatically."

"Bill," Jennifer declared, "I guess I see your point that we're all rich in this country, but Jesus never says money is bad. Some very godly people in the Bible were extremely rich and they got to keep their money!"

Did I hear a hint of desperation?

Now Jennifer's voice hardened. "This is exactly why no one wants to hear sermons on money or giving. Are you trying to make us feel guilty for owning nice things?"

Why is it so hard for a rich person to enter the kingdom of God?

Could the rich man have followed Christ without first giving everything? Explain.

Bill was about to respond when Sue announced proudly, "Jennifer, the Word of God says, 'Money is the root of all evil.'"

Bill opened his mouth but was cut off again, this time by Wayman. "Everybody gets that wrong. It's in 1 Timothy 6:10, and the verse actually says, '**The love of money is a root of all kinds of evil**.' Money's not bad—just the *love* of money."

I marvelled. Was that actually a helpful contribution? From Wayman?

Finally Bill got the chance to speak. "We'll get to that passage in a later class, but I'm glad you clarified the point for this discussion, Wayman." The used car salesman shrugged off Bill's compliment and resumed the frown he had let slip.

"This is part of the answer to Jennifer's question," Bill continued. "If having money and possessions was evil, then we'd all be in trouble. By God's grace, we can use our wealth for tremendous good.

"But let's not minimize the danger of our own selfishness or Satan's efforts. Because we're so wealthy in this country, materialism can easily ensnare us. We can't let down our guard."

More silence. I glanced at Jennifer, but she avoided my look.

Then Cathy said, "Bill, I hope I'm not detracting from your point, but I'm confused. Jesus said the rich man lacked one thing—that is, there was one more thing he had to do. But then Christ gave four commands—sell everything, give to the poor, come, and follow Him."

Bill's whole wrinkled face lit up. "That is a wonderful observation, Cathy. Consider this, that Jesus *did* want the rich man to do one thing, and that one thing was to trust in God instead of in his wealth. Giving everything would have demonstrated and even developed the man's trust in God."

Wayman grumbled, "But if the ruler had given up his riches, he may as well have followed Jesus. There'd be no reason to keep living the way he was."

"Exactly," Bill responded. "There'd be nothing to live for, except for Christ. You see, Jesus wasn't after the man's money—He wanted his heart. In Mark's parallel account we read that '**Jesus looked at him and loved him**.' God is acting in our best interest when He attempts to turn our hearts away from money and toward Himself. When we treasure our money, we reject His love. When we give it all up, we are telling Him we love Him."

Then Bill looked at his Bible before continuing thoughtfully, "In fact, did you happen to notice Jesus' promise…right in the middle of His to-do list?"

"Treasure in heaven," I said. "Jesus told him to exchange his wealth down here for treasure in heaven."

Bill smiled and nodded. "The rich man missed it entirely, didn't he? Not only did Jesus show him the way to eternal life, but He said He *wanted* the man to have treasure—treasure that would last forever!"

Cathy said, "That reminds me of the quote by Jim Elliot, the missionary: 'He is no fool who gives what he cannot keep, to gain what he cannot lose.' In the end, the rewards from God are worth far more than anything we sacrifice."

What does Jesus' phrase **"treasure in heaven"** *mean? How powerfully does the promise of heavenly treasure motivate you?*

Wayman said, "Hey, that's right! After Jesus talked to the rich man, He said that giving stuff up for Christ means we'll get back one hundred times as much. Right now— **'in this age.'** Just think how much richer that guy would have been if he'd just listened to Jesus. That's downright inspiring."

Jennifer nodded vigorously.

"Absolutely not!" Bill exclaimed.

I jumped, and Samantha stifled a smile. Sue coughed.

"Wayman," Bill said, "God longs for us to experience his blessings, but He has much more than earthly riches for us, even in this life. The joy that comes from generosity is worth far more than money."

Bill's face softened. "Please be encouraged. Riches and giving are not easy topics. The battle for our hearts is a fierce one, as the rich young ruler illustrates. We must use wealth for God or it will use us."

He glanced at his watch. "I'll finish today's class by telling you about my good friend Ron. Ron had a wife and two children, and they all attended church regularly. Ron sold real estate successfully and he eventually hired a woman to help show houses to clients. This assistant was young and stunningly attractive. Ron worked long hours, and he and his lovely employee spent a lot of time working side-by-side, just the two of them. They also traveled together to out-of-town realtor conventions."

Bill paused for a moment. His eyes seemed to focus on a scene that none of us could see.

Then he continued, a little distantly. "A friend tried to help Ron see the danger, but Ron downplayed it. He declared his unswerving loyalty to his wife and family. But he was living in denial. Ron refused to admit his sin, even to himself. His affair was finally revealed, and he packed up and left his wife and kids." Tears began to seep into the crevices around Bill's eyes.

Then he took a deep breath and said, "Many of us have fallen into disastrous affairs with wealth. Because our society is so rich, we forget how powerful the allure of wealth is. It's so easy to start serving money instead of God without even realizing it's happening.

"That's exactly what happened with the rich ruler. Jesus' challenge to him amazed the crowd; they thought this man was one of God's model citizens. But the man was deceiving himself and everyone around him. The only person he didn't fool was Jesus. Christ knew that the only remedy was radical action.

"Both Ron and the rich man walked away from Jesus. But I'm still quite close to Ron, and though there was a lot of heartache, I'm overjoyed to say he eventually returned to his family and to his faith in Christ. We don't know if the rich man ever came back to Jesus, but for us his story opens up a treasure chest of wisdom that can lead to unimaginable joy."

What amount of money or which possessions would you be sad to give up? If you gave up that amount of money or if you gave away those possessions, what would be the positive and negative consequences?

Jennifer glanced at the wall clock and Wayman shifted in his chair. It was later than I had realized.

Bill finished abruptly, "See you next week!"

I stood and slowly put on my coat, feeling a mixture of emotions. *Bill's Bible teaching makes a lot of sense, but it's overwhelming. Could my money and possessions be major problems in my life without me even realizing it? How can I know? What can I do?*

I looked around for Jennifer, but she was already gone.

A Brief Debrief

Maybe you're experiencing mixed emotions, as I did when I first met the rich young ruler. I found clearer perspective when I identified three key points from that discussion:

- We are wealthy, even if we rarely feel like it.

- Wealth is dangerous, and we need to keep our guard up.

- Acting with joyful generosity from God is the best way to confront and resist these dangers.

If you are coming out of this lesson feeling guilty, I encourage you to meditate on Romans 8:1: "**Therefore, there is now no condemnation for those who are in Christ Jesus.**" If you examine your heart before God, you'll find that either your guilt is *false*—you haven't done anything wrong—or it is *real,* and complete forgiveness from Christ is readily available.

On earth, when someone is convicted of a crime, he loses his freedom. But when God convicts us, we have the opportunity to confess and change our behaviour, gaining freedom in Christ. Jesus said, "**If you hold to my teaching, you are really my disciples. Then you will know the truth, and the truth will set you free**" (John 8:31-32).

Instead of focusing on the money and possessions you haven't shared, start to live generously now, and build a foundation of obedience that you can look back on with joy.

---

*"**Sell everything you have and give to the poor, and you will have treasure in heaven. Then come, follow me**" (Luke 18:22). If God said this to you, how eagerly would you listen? Would you do it? Why or why not?*

Deeper Study

1. In the Parable of the Sower (Mark 4), Jesus taught, "**Still others, like seed sown among thorns, hear the word; but the worries of this life, the deceitfulness of wealth and the desires for other things come in and choke the word, making it unfruitful**" (verses 18-19). What more does this teach you about the dangers of wealth?

2. Psalm 24: 1 says, "**The earth is the LORD's, and everything in it, the world, and all who live in it**." Do you act as if you believe this? If so, explain your answer. If not, what would it take for you to believe this at the very core of your being?

Please Welcome Tonight's Keynote Speaker, Zacchaeus!

WE WERE GIVING EACH OTHER the silent treatment as we sat in the noisy café. Jennifer sat stiffly in her chair, alternating between drawn-out sips from her coffee and nervous glances at everyone who came through the doorway. Twice she started to speak, only to return her full attention to her cup and the Saturday night crowd.

Finally, she blurted out, "I don't know if I want to attend the class anymore, Joe."

I fished for words. She wouldn't meet my eyes.

Before I could speak, Jennifer continued, "The class isn't what I expected. I want to learn how to be a well-rounded steward of my money, but the class is impractical and unfocused. Bill is warm and sincere, but he's not results-oriented. I wonder how he ever managed a bakery!" She rolled her eyes, still avoiding mine, then took another sip with forced nonchalance.

More pompously than I intended, I said, "I seem to remember *someone* saying something about finishing what they start." Jennifer's glare told me I'd gone too far.

At least she's looking me in the eye, I thought.

I hastened to smooth the tension. "I have to admit that I was offended at times." A thoughtful pause, then, "But, you know, I haven't been able to get Jesus' words to the rich ruler out of my head. I'm still not sure what I'm supposed to do about it…"

When she didn't respond, I pressed further, "How about giving it just another week or two, Jenn? What do you say?"

She waited a long time before responding. "The class seems so impractical." Why did I think she was skirting the real issue? "We need specific suggestions on how to run our financial affairs and avoid debt. The world is so confusing. Christians need to know what to do."

"That's similar to what the rich man said," I mused. "He wanted to know what to do, but he didn't like Jesus' response."

The room temperature instantly dropped five degrees. We finished our coffee in silence.

*　　*　　*

That Sunday the class members filed in warily. Wayman arrived last, obviously preoccupied, for people had to keep repeating themselves when they spoke to him. I was pleased that Jennifer had decided to continue attending the class after all.

We prayed. Then Bill said, "Could one or two people summarize some of the points we covered last week?"

Cathy spoke up first, "What struck me was how wealthy we are. I worry so much about my family having enough, but we always have much more than our daily bread."

"And don't forget the dangers of riches," Mrs. Coyne added. "Our Lord taught, '**Indeed, it is easier for a camel to go through the eye of a needle than for a rich man to enter the kingdom of God**.' We've underestimated what a trap too much money is."

"I think we're overreacting," Jennifer said. "If being wealthy is so precarious for our faith, wouldn't prominent Christian leaders be strongly warning us?"

I was surprised when Samantha responded, "Isn't Jesus a prominent Christian leader?"

Jennifer raised her eyebrows at Samantha. No one spoke for several seconds.

Reverend Moss teaches against materialism, I thought. His sermon on generosity got me into this class too.

Finally, Bill made an awkward attempt to recover the conversation, "Thank you for your comments." He glanced at his notes, then continued with fresh determination, "Now, let's turn to the story of Zacchaeus, which Luke closely links to the story of the rich ruler. In fact, the two stories are only thirteen verses apart."

He shifted in his chair and asked, "Wayman, would you please read our main passage...Luke 19:1-10?"

The pre-owned vehicle salesman nodded vaguely, his mind apparently somewhere else. Then he blinked twice, sat up straighter and read,

> **[1]Jesus entered Jericho and was passing through. [2]A man was there by the name of Zacchaeus; he was a chief tax collector and was wealthy. [3]He wanted to see who Jesus was, but being a short man he could not, because of the crowd. [4]So he ran ahead and climbed a sycamore-fig tree to see him, since Jesus was coming that way.**
>
> **[5]When Jesus reached the spot, he looked up and said to him, "Zacchaeus,**

come down immediately. I must stay at
your house today." ⁶So he came down at
once and welcomed him gladly.
⁷All the people saw this and began to
mutter, "He has gone to be the guest of a
'sinner.'"
⁸But Zacchaeus stood up and said to
the Lord, "Look, Lord! Here and now I
give half of my possessions to the poor,
and if I have cheated anybody out of anything, I will pay back four times the
amount."
⁹Jesus said to him, "Today salvation
has come to this house, because this man,
too, is a son of Abraham. ¹⁰For the Son of
Man came to seek and to save what was
lost."

Bill said, "Luke placed this passage only a few verses after
the story of the rich ruler so that his readers would compare
and contrast the two figures. They have many similarities
and differences. They were both wealthy. They also both
held positions of influence, although the ruler was respected and Zacchaeus was despised."

"Just like today," I muttered. "Nobody likes the tax
agent. The passage says Zacchaeus was a *chief* tax collec-
tor, so I guess he would have been even richer than any of
those other thieves."

Bill laughed. "Joe, since you already have the floor,
would you read the passage for us a second time?"

As soon as I had finished,
Bill asked the group, "First, what
did Zacchaeus give up?"

*How are you similar to and
different from Zacchaeus?
Do you relate more closely
to him or to the rich ruler?*

"A lot!" Cathy said. "He
promised to repay four times the
amount he cheated people out of."

"And...?" Bill prompted.

"And he gave fully half of his money and possessions to the poor!"

Mrs. Coyne looked over her glasses at Bill, eyebrows raised. "Are you trying to say that we should give away fifty percent of our money?"

"This passage is not about a specific percentage, Sue," our leader answered. "God doesn't focus on such formulas, especially in the New Testament, because He doesn't want us to become legalistic. The Old Testament Law set out tithing and offering requirements, but few Israelites ever followed those laws. Many who did, like the Pharisees, completely missed the intent of the laws—namely, to show us how to love God and His people."

Wayman cut in, "So this tax guy cheated people, huh?" He stared absently toward the window.

Jennifer sat up straight and began to lecture, "In Israel at that time, tax collection was like an extortion racket. The Roman government hired tax collectors from among the Jewish people, and Roman soldiers enforced their authority. Therefore, tax collectors had almost free rein to extort large amounts for their own pockets. They were reviled as both cheaters and traitors."

Bill nodded in agreement, but he was watching Wayman closely.

"So let's say..." Wayman scratched his beard. "Let's say he got ten percent of his money from cheating. Four times ten percent..." he squinted as he calculated, oblivious to the rest of us, "that's forty percent. Then add the fifty percent for the poor. That means he gave up almost...," he trailed off and looked down quickly.

"Almost everything he had," Bill finished gently. "In fact, depending on how much of a crook he was, Zacchaeus may very well have promised to give up *more* than he had. Zacchaeus actually fulfilled Jesus' command to the rich young man, and certainly with much greater enthusiasm."

I sat stunned. *Ridiculous! The man got caught up in the moment, trying to impress the famous rabbi. Surely he wouldn't actually follow through on his promises? What kind of stewardship would that be?*

Mrs. Coyne interrupted my musing. "But the people he cheated would have been amazed just to get back what they lost—that would be a miracle in itself! Why would he give it all when he didn't have to?"

"Indeed," Bill agreed. "Why did Zacchaeus do all this?"

"Clearly he didn't consult a certified financial planner," Jennifer deadpanned. Everyone laughed.

"Seriously, though," Jennifer continued, "I would have advised him against it. He might wipe himself out financially. What would he do then? And which poor would he give to? Were the gifts tax deductible?"

Cathy joined in, "And what about his family's needs and his savings for retirement?"

"Good questions, all," Bill answered. "Neither Zacchaeus nor Jesus mentioned these issues, did they?"

"He probably just wanted the publicity, like all those celebrities today," Mrs. Coyne speculated. She opened her Bible and consulted it. "However, I know boasting is wrong. In Matthew 6:3, Jesus said, '**But when you give to the needy, do not let your left hand know what your right hand is doing.**' Zacchaeus was a showoff!"

Cathy flipped to the same passage. "I'm not sure that

FYI: *The religious lawmakers of the day often limited gifts to 20% of one's income. Zacchaeus noisily flouted this regulation when he gave 50% of what he owned to the poor. The Mosaic Law (Leviticus 6:1-5; Numbers 5:5-7) required a thief to return the amount stolen plus 20% as a penalty. Zacchaeus owed his victims only 120%, but he vowed to pay back 400%.*

Why did Zacchaeus give away and repay so much?

Was Zacchaeus practicing wise financial stewardship? Do you think he would come to regret his decision?

36

teaching applies here, Sue. In Matthew 6, Jesus criticized the hypocrites because of their wrong motivation. They gave in order to be honoured by men. Zacchaeus made his promise as a toast to his Messiah. See? Jesus immediately announced his salvation and called Zacchaeus a son of Abraham."

"That was the highest compliment a Jew could receive," Bill added.

"It sounds like Zacchaeus traded his money for salvation," I said, only half-joking. "He bought God off!"

"I don't think so," Samantha answered. I was struck by the soft simplicity of her tone. "This was a gift. I think Zacchaeus was desperate for love. It says here that he welcomed Jesus gladly. He *wanted* to give. He was changed now, and money didn't matter any more." Suddenly she looked down and adjusted her glasses. "Well, anyway, that's the way it seems to me."

Bill spoke to all of us, but kept smiling toward Samantha. "The more we understand God's love toward us, the more we want to respond in obedience—in generosity. And, I might add, the more we obey and give, the more we grow in love toward God."

Jennifer cleared her throat. "Yeah, but can't you do that without giving everything away? Can't you show a change of heart by saying, 'Lord, I give you my trust, my heart'?"

Bill responded, "If Zacchaeus had only done that, would Jesus have responded the

> How were Zacchaeus's actions related to his salvation?

same way?" When no one answered, he continued, "Zacchaeus's public commitment made it clear that his heart had changed, and Jesus validated that fact. I think Zacchaeus needed to take that radical step as much to convince himself as to convince anyone else.

"The rich ruler from last week would undoubtedly have paid lip service to Psalm 24:1, '**The earth is the LORD's,**

and everything in it,' but Zacchaeus *lived* it. A lot of people are willing to give God credit, but so few will give Him cash!"

A few of us laughed.

Bill went on, "That leads to my next question: For rich people like us, how is giving related to heart change?"

"Well," Jennifer said, "we're not supposed to give at all if our hearts are not in the right place or if we feel pushed into it. Second Corinthians 9:7 says, '**Each man should give what he has decided in his heart to give, not reluctantly or under compulsion, for God loves a cheerful giver.**'"

Mrs. Coyne nodded. Wayman examined his bejewelled hands.

Samantha opened then closed her mouth. Then she said, "Well, I don't know the Bible very well, and I'm sure you have a good point, Jennifer," she took a deep breath, "but in our first meeting we talked about how our heart follows our treasure. I mean, maybe there are times when we should do the right thing first, and then we'll feel better about it later."

That took guts, I thought.

"Maybe Zacchaeus's heart changed even before he announced his plans," Jennifer suggested.

"Jesus didn't proclaim his salvation until *after* Zacchaeus made the verbal commitment," Cathy said gently.

In the silence that followed, Bill glanced around the room. "You all look more like that mournful rich man than like Zacchaeus." That drew a few wry smiles. "How about if we leave it at this: Whether Zach's heart changed before or after, we know that joy accompanied his ridiculously generous gifts. So now let's move on to my last question: Does he regret his decision?"

Jennifer responded, "He might have regretted it later when the poor harassed him for donations and every Joe

38

and his brother showed up to claim restitution. Plus, his lifestyle would take a huge hit."

"True, but what about now? Present tense. As we speak, does Zacchaeus regret his decision?"

The answer dawned on me suddenly. I blurted out, "Zacchaeus is in heaven right now. He will be there for all eternity, worshiping the Lord and enjoying his treasure. No regrets there..."

My voice trailed off, because I was surprised to see a single tear rolling down Wayman's cheek and disappearing into his thin beard. He quickly wiped it away with a motion disguised as a stretch. I looked around the room, but everyone else was still watching me. Except Bill, who shot a furtive glance in Wayman's direction.

Jennifer pressed her lips together and shook her head. "This all seems so vague. How much does God want us to give?"

Bill answered, "There's no bar we have to reach. The rich man would have parted with any *reasonable* amount Jesus named. On the other hand, Zacchaeus gave unreasonably, well beyond what was required. He gave with joyful generosity."

"Bill," I said, "I give until it hurts, but I have a very low pain threshold. How can I possibly be eager to give everything?"

Do you think that giving freely and generously is either imprudent or impossible?

Bill smiled. "Give until it *doesn't* hurt—until it's freeing. Give until you can't wait to share. Then God's joy will overflow in your life."

Some say, "Give until it hurts." Where is your giving pain threshold?

Jennifer said, "I'm not sure that we should focus on giving everything." My girlfriend had her Bible open. "First Corinthians 13, the love chapter, says, '**If I give all I possess to the poor and surrender my body to the flames, but have not love, I gain nothing.**' God wants us to love Him, plain and simple. The focus is on love, not on giving."

Bill said, "That's true, Jennifer. Perhaps we have been focusing too much on giving... God's love is the goal. Period. But in our society, isn't giving one of the best ways to express love to God? Giving also helps us to detach from our earthly treasure so God can fill our hearts with more of His love."

He looked around the circle. "Does giving seem like a downer to you? In view of Jesus' love and mercy, Zacchaeus was thrilled to offer his sacrifice. One way to express the joy of our salvation is to give. And the more we give, the more we find joy in trusting and knowing our Lord and in knowing that we have heavenly treasure awaiting us. Money becomes almost meaningless compared to Christ's love and mercy.

"Do we hesitate to give because we don't want to let go of our stuff, like that sad rich man? Or are we so overcome by joy that we can't wait to be generous, like Zacchaeus? Do we see sacrificial giving as unreasonable? Or do we see giving as an expression of love to our Saviour and an investment in true, heavenly treasure?"

How strongly does each of the following motivate you to give and share?

- *Desire to obey God*
- *Desire to trust God more*
- *Treasure in heaven*
- *Anything else*

Bill paused, then glanced at his watch. "Our time is up for today. During the coming week, think about this question: What action will I take in light of the stories of the rich ruler and Zacchaeus?"

Action? I wondered. *What does Bill expect us to do? Give away everything we have?* I found all of this discussion stimulating, but I still didn't know what to *do* about it.

A couple of minutes later, Jennifer and I were walking toward my car when I realized that I had left my favourite coffee cup sitting under my chair. I hurried back to the room and was about to turn into the doorway when I heard Wayman's voice inside. I stopped short.

"Oh, never mind," I heard him say. "I wasn't serious."

I peeked around the doorjamb and saw that Wayman and Bill were alone in the room, and Bill has holding something out to Wayman.

"A deal's a deal," said Bill. "You came to three classes, as you promised. Now I'm keeping my end. Here's the cheque for the car. You have no obligation to set foot in this classroom ever again."

Wayman looked down, shoulders hunched, and scuffed the carpet with the toe of his boot. Then he reached out slowly and took the cheque. "Well, I have no idea why you want to buy a car you don't need."

"Oh, I'm sure there will be a need for it. And, by the way, could I ask you to keep it for me a while longer?"

"What? Oh, yeah, I guess so." Wayman turned partway toward the door, then back. "I have to tell you, Bill—and don't you ever tell anyone I said this." He waited until Bill responded with a nod. "I, uh… Well, you got me thinking, okay? So I might just come back again. Just one more week. Or two, maybe."

"I'd enjoy that, Wayman," Bill said.

Then Wayman strode through the door so quickly that I couldn't back away in time, and we bumped into each other. Wayman stepped back and gave me a long, calculating look. Then he said gruffly, "Somebody's got to stick around to talk some sense into this class!" He stumped off down the hall.

I watched him until he was out of sight, then I slunk into the room to retrieve my cup. Bill and I eyed each other silently. Cup in hand, not knowing what to say, I simply wished Bill a good day and started to leave.

"Joe," he said to my back. I stopped, still facing the door. "There's no need for anyone else to know what you just heard."

"Sure," I replied over my shoulder. Then I hurried to catch up with Jennifer.

A Brief Debrief

I remember experiencing some confusion that day, but I now understand that, while money can be dangerous, it is also a valuable tool when we entrust it to God.

Zacchaeus's story left me with three key principles:

- Money and possessions are worthless when compared to Jesus.

- Joy over Christ's love and grace motivates us to share our wealth.

- Even if we don't feel generous, it's best to give anyway. By giving, we store up treasure in heaven. We also actively transfer our trust from our wealth to our Saviour.

What Zacchaeus did may seem foolish, but take to heart a few questions: What might be required for you to become free from materialism and to learn the joy of generosity as he did? Who else might need your possessions more than you do? Which of your possessions have sat unused for years, and which have become useless burdens? Which of your expenses could you replace with giving—even just for a month?

When Zacchaeus announced his commitment, he became accountable to those who heard. Ask one or more trusted friends or your small group to hold you accountable for your handling of money and possessions. This might be especially important if generosity doesn't come easily to you.

(You'll note that in our group's first meeting, everyone expected to learn something different about money: how to stay out of debt, how to save, how to teach children to be wise financially, etc. Then, before our third meeting, Jennifer said she wanted to learn to be a "well-rounded" steward of money. Now, our study series did address debt, savings, and all the various money topics. But it's not well-rounded or balanced, because the Bible itself isn't balanced. When God's Word refers to money and possessions, it most often tells us not to be attached to our earthly treasure. The Bible frequently talks about giving too.)

Is it possible for a rich person to be close to God without giving joyfully and freely?

What action will you take in light of the stories of the rich ruler and Zacchaeus?

Tithing:
Our Financial
Foundation?

I HAD DRIVEN PAST WAYMAN'S gaudily-decorated car lot many times, but this was the first time I had ever driven onto the property. Brashly coloured flags, balloons, and signs shouted for my attention. I drove past the shiny, newer cars on display near the entrance and found a parking spot near the dingier-looking vehicles that sat several rows back from the street.

No fewer than three hungry-eyed salesmen accosted me on my way to Wayman's office. For a moment I even toyed with the trade-in offer one of them made for my own car, but then I remembered why I was here.

Through his open office door, I could see Wayman talking animatedly on the phone. He spotted me and beckoned me in. I sat in one of two chairs on the near side of his desk.

"No, I told you Friday is too late," Wayman said loudly into the receiver. "I have a customer already who expects delivery by Wednesday." He paused. "No, I can't tell him that. I made—" he glanced uncomfortably at me, then continued more solemnly, "I made a promise. I plan to keep it."

With that he hung up the phone, crossed the room quickly to close the door, then returned and sat behind his desk. After fiddling for a moment with a cheap stick pen that said "Best Deal in Town" on one side, Wayman sighed deeply and said, "Joe, this wasn't my plan. I called Bill to...to talk about the class. And he told me to talk with you instead."

"Me?" My curiosity about the reason for Wayman's invitation was only growing deeper. "Bill's the expert on the Bible and money stuff. Why would he send you to me?"

"Well, he said I needed an accountability partner. He suggested you."

"Accountability? For what?"

Wayman swivelled in his chair and stared through the office's side window. The view was dominated by polished chrome and sparkling clean windshields.

"For so long, I've lived my life for painted sheet metal...cast iron...white-walled rubber...and money." He sighed again. "My whole career I've done whatever it took to make the sale." A grimace, then a soft chuckle. "Then I met Zacchaeus, my twin."

I began to realize a miracle had occurred.

Still gazing out the window, Wayman continued, "I've never been happy. I've been selfish—and dishonest. And I never realized how heavy the burden had become...until last Sunday, when Jesus told me I could be free. When we read that story and Jesus talked to Zacchaeus...He was talking to me." Tears began to well in Wayman's eyes, and he said in a rush, "God's done so much for me, maybe I'll give it all away."

"Everything?" I blurted incredulously. "You're going to give everything away?"

"I don't know." He swiped quickly at his cheeks. "Maybe not everything, like Zacchaeus, but it has to be drastic. Maybe some free cars for poor people. Or maybe I'll go through my invoices and give some customers back their money. Or something." He giggled through his tears. "I don't know what to do, but it feels so good. It's crazy!" He giggled again, louder and longer.

Wayman's mood was contagious and I started to laugh with him. But as my volume rose, Wayman stopped suddenly and looked at me awkwardly, as though seeing me for the first time. He pulled a handkerchief from his pants pocket and hastily dried his face.

"Well, anyway," he said. "I guess I need someone to—you know—pray for me…and make sure I don't change my mind."

"I'd be honoured," I replied.

Wayman played with the stick pen again, then looked me in the eye, contrition written on his face. "I'm new at this, Joe. So I guess maybe, if it's okay with you, we should meet once a week or something."

"That's fine with me. I'm free this same time next week."

"Great." He smiled. "That's great. Uh, thanks, Joe."

"Hey, no problem." I rose to leave. "And I promise to be praying for you every day."

"Oh, and Joe?" Wayman's eyes flicked to the window, then the door. "Can we just keep this between you and me? And Bill?"

"You bet, my friend."

We shook hands, and I returned to my car.

*   *   *

I knew Bill was going to ask, and he didn't disappoint me, but I still didn't have an answer.

"I'd like to hear what you've done with last week's homework question: What action will you take in light of the stories of the rich young ruler and Zacchaeus?" We had just finished praying, and these were the first words out of Bill's mouth.

During the long silence that followed, I looked at Wayman, who gave me first a nervous frown, then a faint smile. *Small consolation that the used car salesman has gone farther with this than I have.*

Finally, Bill let us off the hook. "This is a very personal question and sometimes it takes time to determine the direction of our obedience. So it's understandable if no one has an answer."

He glanced down at his notes. "All right, then, today's topic is tithing. *Tithe* means 'ten percent,' and many Christians believe this is the portion of our income we should give to God. I've chosen four key passages on the topic.

"The first is Genesis 14:17-20. God had just given Abram victory in battle over a wicked king named Kedorlaomer and his allies."

Bill looked to his left. "Now then, Sue, do you mind reading for us?"

So Mrs. Coyne read,

> [17]After Abram returned from defeating Kedorlaomer and the kings allied with him, the king of Sodom came out to meet him in the Valley of Shaveh (that is, the King's Valley).
> [18]Then Melchizedek king of Salem brought out bread and wine. He was priest of God Most High, [19]and he blessed Abram, saying,
>
> > "Blessed be Abram by God Most High,
> > Creator of heaven and earth.

**[20]And blessed be God Most High,
who delivered your enemies into
your hand."**

**Then Abram gave him a tenth of every-
thing.**

After the second reading, Bill said, "This Abram is the
same man God later renamed 'Abraham,' the father of the
Jewish nation. What, then, does this passage say to us about
tithing?"

Jennifer answered, "Tithing is commanded in God's
Law in Leviticus, Numbers, and Deuteronomy. Some people argue that these laws are no longer in force. However,
even if this is true, the tithe started before the Law: Abram
gave his tithe before God gave the Law to the Israelites.
Therefore, it's still valid today, unless the New Testament
specifically revokes it, which it never does. Abram sets a
clear example for us here, so I'm firmly in favour of tithing."

"But, young lady," said Mrs. Coyne, "God never commanded Abram to tithe. In fact, Abram made many offerings to God, but this is the only time a percentage is mentioned. Paul doesn't teach the tithe, either; he says to give
by grace, not by law.

"Personally, I'm beginning to think the tithe is legalistic, and if church leaders try to force it on us, we'll just be
fulfilling cold, hard regulations."

"But don't you think the rules are there for a reason?"
Wayman surprised us with the question. "I mean, you can
be legalistic about anything the Bible teaches. It's all how
you look at it. Are you doing it just to keep a dead rule, or
to get close to God?"

"I appreciate your perspective, Wayman," said Bill.
Wayman gave a jerky nod. "So, according to the passage,
what was Abram's motive for tithing?"

"It doesn't say," I answered. "No one told Abram to tithe, so his giving seems to have been from internal motivation—just something he decided to do, like Zacchaeus did."

After a moment, Samantha said, "Abram was thankful. God helped him win the battle, and the priest—Mel...chi...zedek?—well, the priest gave Abram that wonderful message from God. So Abram was just saying thank you to the Lord." She pushed her glasses back with one finger. "And besides, he knew that *all* his money was God's. Abram was just taking care of God's stuff for Him, and he knew God would make sure he had what he needed."

"That's right," said Wayman gruffly. "This week I talked to Rev. Moss about tithing. He said that one tenth of our money stands for the whole thing, and when we give a tenth, we're really saying, 'It's all yours, God.' But maybe a tenth isn't enough to help some people remember that—especially for rich people like us."

Eyes popped and jaws dropped all around the circle. Even I marvelled to hear Wayman speak this way.

Why do you think Abram gave a tithe?

But Jennifer squinted skeptically. "Then what's enough, Wayman?"

The car dealer began to squirm. "How should I know?" He looked down at his hands. That's when I noticed he was wearing only a simple wedding band and an inexpensive watch.

"I'd say that's a good lead-in to our second passage, from the Law of Moses," Bill suggested. "Jennifer, you're next to read, if you don't mind—Leviticus 27:30-34."

Jennifer read,

30"A tithe of everything from the land, whether grain from the soil or fruit from

the trees, belongs to the LORD; it is holy to
the LORD. ³¹If a man redeems any of his
tithe, he must add a fifth of the value to it.
³²The entire tithe of the herd and flock—
every tenth animal that passes under the
shepherd's rod—will be holy to the LORD.
³³He must not pick out the good from the
bad or make any substitution. If he does
make a substitution, both the animal and
its substitute become holy and cannot be
redeemed."
³⁴These are the commands the LORD
gave Moses on Mount Sinai for the Israelites.

"See?" Jennifer added. "This is the last command in the
whole book of Leviticus; God wanted to leave his people
with the memory of a very important practice. We are required to tithe."

"But—" Mrs. Coyne pointed to her Bible, "did you notice the last three words: 'for the Israelites'? These laws
aren't for us."

Jennifer's voice became dan-
gerously smooth. "Okay, but
God still owns everything, and
giving a tenth still serves to re-

*Do the commands in Leviti-
cus 27:30-34 apply to us
today?*

mind us of that. That's why the passage says that the tithe
of all a person's income belongs to God."

"Yeah," I said, feeling puzzled, "but the government
automatically takes a huge piece of our paycheques. Then
there are all sorts of other deductions, many of them mandatory. Should we pay the tithe on our income before taxes
and deductions, or afterwards?"

Jennifer had done her homework. "Before taxes, Joe. In
Deuteronomy 26, Numbers 18:12, and many other passages, the Bible says to give the *firstfruits*—that is, the first

and best portion of the harvest. We must take our tithe right off the top, before any expenses."

Cathy had been silent, but at this she shook her head firmly and said, "For most of us, the government takes its cut before we see any money at all, so taxes aren't really ours to begin with. I can't image trying to tithe on money Bob and I never bring home. Besides, what about all the businesspeople who have high expenses for running their businesses? Take Bill's bakery, for instance. I'm sure most of the money that customers paid Bill went to staff salaries, equipment, rent, and so on—"

"I mentioned that it takes a lot of dough to make bread, didn't I?" Bill smiled benignly. We all winced.

Undeterred by the interjection, Cathy continued, "Any tithe Bill gave wouldn't come out of his income *before* these expenses, would it? The tithe would come out of his income after expenses, out of the profit. So what's the difference between deductions for running a business and deductions for running a government?"

"So why not also deduct the expenses for running my life?" responded Jennifer. "By your reasoning, I should deduct my rent, my car payments, my clothes—basically everything—before figuring the tithe. And the way I— Well, I mean, the way *some* people spend, that would leave nothing to tithe on."

Bill jumped in, "Very good insights. Let's move along to Malachi 3:6-12. Would you read it for us, Samantha?"

Samantha nodded. Her grandmother helped her find Malachi, and with several pauses she read,

⁶"I the LORD do not change. So you, O descendants of Jacob, are not destroyed. ⁷Ever since the time of your forefathers you have turned away from my decrees and have not kept them. Return to me, and I will return to you," says the LORD Almighty.

"But you ask, 'How are we to return?' ⁸"Will a man rob God? Yet you rob me.

"But you ask, 'How do we rob you?'

"In tithes and offerings. ⁹You are under a curse—the whole nation of you—because you are robbing me. ¹⁰Bring the whole tithe into the storehouse, that there may be food in my house. Test me in this," says the LORD Almighty, "and see if I will not throw open the floodgates of heaven and pour out so much blessing that you will not have room enough for it. ¹¹I will prevent pests from devouring your crops, and the vines in your fields will not cast their fruit," says the LORD Almighty. ¹²"Then all the nations will call you blessed, for yours will be a delightful land," says the LORD Almighty.

"Don't you see?" demanded Jennifer. "'**The whole tithe.**' Anything less is robbing God. But if we give God his due, we will be blessed beyond imagining!"

"Young lady," Mrs. Coyne scolded, "you sound just like a preacher for that Health and Wealth Gospel! God doesn't want us to give just to get more. That's greedy. Anyways, it doesn't work that way today. Lots of people give faithfully and stay poor. We're under the New Covenant, and this passage is part of the Old Covenant."

I broke in. "Bill, what's this *storehouse* the passage talks about?"

"It's the part of the temple where people brought their offerings," Bill answered. "It represents the place of worship and spiritual leadership."

"That raises another question," I said. "Does this mean we can only tithe to our local church—our place of worship today? What about supporting parachurch ministries and missionaries from other churches? I have friends overseas, and I'd like to give them part of my tithe."

Before Bill could answer, Jennifer replied, "It's clear here that the place of worship is where the whole tithe goes. Anything above the tithe can go to other ministries. Of course, our local church should be dedicating a good portion of its budget to missions and feeding the hungry anyway. So church giving helps those ministries too."

> **FYI:** *In the Old Testament, the Israelites may have been required to give three different tithes: (1) the Priest's Tithe to support the work of the Levites (Numbers 18:21); (2) the Festival Tithe, which the giver ate himself to celebrate God's blessings (Deuteronomy 14:22-27); and (3) the Poor Tithe, which went to the poor every third year (Deuteronomy 14:28-29, although this may have been simply a redirection of the Festival Tithe every third year). So, a faithful Israelite actually tithed between twenty and twenty-three percent per year, and voluntary "offerings" came on top of that.*

Samantha spoke up bravely. "But Jesus told the rich ruler to give everything to the poor. Zacchaeus never mentioned the storehouses, and Jesus said he was doing the right thing giving half his money to the poor."

Jennifer came right back. "The Malachi passage says, '**I the LORD do not change**.' Then He made clear that tithing was very important to Him. Even if we're not technically under the Law anymore, God's decrees are still very good. We are robbing God if we don't tithe."

"Robbing God…" Cathy tapped her chin. "For the rich young ruler, it wasn't an issue of keeping a particular law, but an issue of the heart and its devotion. No doubt he gave his tithes and offerings regularly, yet that was not enough. He was robbing God by treating the remaining ninety percent as his own. So maybe it's possible for us to rob God even if we are tithing."

"That's ridiculous." Jennifer crossed her arms. "If you're tithing, you're not robbing God."

"Actually, Jennifer," Bill pointed out, "God told Israel that they weren't giving their tithes *and offerings*. He expected more than just ten percent from them. But I respect the points you've made.

Are we robbing God if we don't tithe?

Do God's promises in the Malachi passage apply to us today? If so, what blessings can we expect if we give generously?

"Now, before we run out of time, let's let Jesus weigh in on tithing. Matthew 23 consists entirely of a very harsh speech by Jesus, condemning the Pharisees and the teachers of the Law. The Pharisees were part of the religious ruling council and many Jews respected the Pharisees for their education and adherence to the Mosaic Law. Joe, would you please read verses 23-24?"

I read,

> **23"Woe to you, teachers of the law and Pharisees, you hypocrites! You give a tenth of your spices—mint, dill and cummin. But you have neglected the more important matters of the law—justice, mercy and faithfulness. You should have practiced the latter, without neglecting the former. 24You blind guides! You strain out a gnat but swallow a camel."**

Bill added, "The tithe is mentioned in only three other places in the New Testament, but without much direct teaching on it. What did Jesus say about the tithe here?"

"He upheld it," Jennifer said. "He accused the Pharisees of neglecting justice, mercy and faithfulness, but He also said not to neglect tithing."

FYI: *Elsewhere in the New Testament, tithing is mentioned only in Luke 11:42; 18:12; and Hebrews 7:2-9.*

"I wonder why Jesus hardly ever mentioned tithing?" asked Cathy. "He certainly had plenty of opportunities."

"And the amount they gave wasn't even His main point here," offered Wayman. "These Pharisee guys were just being legalistic. They made a big deal about the little things and missed what was really important."

"They majored in the minors," I said. "You know, I can see how a solid number or formula can be good for people. All of us need good, clear goals. Sometimes, though, too big a focus on goals can distract us from God's true priorities."

In your own words, describe the central issue Jesus addressed in verses 23-24 of Matthew 23. Why did He mention tithing here?

Why didn't Jesus give clearer instructions about tithing?

Wayman grunted, then said in a low voice, "If you ask me, giving just a tenth is downright cheap, especially for rich folks like us." He glanced around the room. "Not that I'm pushing for any kind of radical change or anything, mind you."

I smiled to myself. Wayman is learning a lot. Then I cringed, realizing the implications for myself. He thinks giving ten percent is cheap? What would that make me, then? The ultimate miser?

Jennifer wasn't satisfied. "But that still leaves the question of how much we are required to give God. Ten percent is a solid, biblical number. Bill, you've been awfully quiet. Do you think we need to give a ten-percent tithe?"

Bill grinned. "I'll answer that and summarize today's study at the same time, Jennifer. God blessed Abram and, apparently without being told to, Abram gave a tithe to God. God then made the tithe a crucial part of the Law of Moses, but the Israelites often didn't obey the laws, bringing trouble for their nation. In Malachi, God told the people of Israel they were under a curse because the nation was robbing Him of tithes and offerings. The Lord promised Israel unbelievable blessings if they would bring the whole tithe into the storehouse. In the New Testament, curiously, the tithe is barely mentioned. In fact, Jesus severely criticized the Pharisees and Law-teachers despite their scrupulous tithing.

"As Sue mentioned, we are now under grace, not law. But some of us use that as an excuse to give less. In truth, God's grace—His lavish, undeserved giving to us—should so overwhelm us that we don't put any boundaries on our own giving and sharing.

"Now, under the New Covenant of grace, even if tithing is no longer required, it's still a great idea. I told you before about my friend Ron. Well, Ron was a heavy drinker in his day. Once he was traveling overseas, in a country where it was legal to drive drunk. He got in a terrible accident and learned the hard way that it was still wise to drive sober. Many people—especially people who are still learning to give—need a yardstick. That's the tithe. But when they graduate past that most basic goal, that's when they will start experiencing incredible joy and won't want to stop."

I broke in, "So maybe we should think of the tithe as the minimum for giving."

"Perhaps," Bill responded, "although I don't like the word *minimum*. It implies that the remaining ninety percent is our own. The reality is that God graciously lets us use *His* wealth for a while before we have to leave it all behind.

"Rich people like us can easily live on less than ninety percent of our incomes, so I challenge everyone here—including myself—to give and share more than ten percent of our incomes. If generous giving is difficult for you, consider why that might be. Do you really believe that everything belongs to God? Does your desire for Him outshine your desire for things?

Discuss one or both of these questions only if the discussion will help you toward joyful generosity:

Should we tithe on our gross income (before taxes and deductions) or net income (after taxes and deductions)?

Is it appropriate to give part of our tithe directly to the poor, to parachurch ministries or to missionaries?

"Dwell often and long on all that God has given you—every material blessing you enjoy every day, and the eternal life and heavenly blessing you will enjoy through all eternity. If that's your focus, then giving will be a natural expression of your overflowing gratitude."

Bill took a deep breath. "Thank you all for the lively discussion. In addition to reading next week's passage, your homework is simply to pray for one other person in the group, that they might become rich toward God."

Pray for someone else? I thought. I think I need to pray for myself too.

Suddenly curious, I pulled out my class schedule and looked ahead one week. It read "The Sermon on the Amount." Somehow I suspected it wasn't a misprint.

A Brief Debrief

We ended our tithing discussion with several questions unanswered. But I was beginning to become firmly convinced of a few key principles that were completely clear:

- No matter how much we give, we must recognize that everything we have is God's.

- In the Old Testament, the tithe represented the whole of one's income. This is still a very helpful principle for us today, reminding us of God's complete ownership.

- Our *purpose* in tithing is far more important than the way we calculate the tithe.

- Tithing should be the *foundation,* not the ceiling, of our giving.

Whole books have been written about tithing, and I encourage you to check them out, but my purpose here is to focus on the more basic questions, such as, What is my motivation for giving at any level? God told Israel that one of the purposes of the tithing process was "**so that you may learn to revere the Lord your God always**" (Deuteronomy 14:23).

Indeed, tithing and giving are forms of worship. That's why Israel tithed at the temple, their centre of worship. The principle still holds true today. Wherever or however you give, are you expressing reverence to God? Which master are you serving by your attitudes toward money and the ways you use it?

Does God want you to tithe? If you do not tithe, consider: How might tithing change your life, for better or worse?

Whatever your level of giving, examine your heart before God. Does your giving express love for God and people? Do you see any signs of greed or self-indulgence inside yourself? (Forgiveness and inner change are readily available—1 John 1:9.)

Deeper Study

Tithing is not unique to the Bible. It was a common practice throughout many ancient cultures. To learn more about the Old Testament's teaching on tithing, study some or all of these passages (in addition to the four main passages in the chapter): Genesis 28:22; Numbers 18; Deuteronomy 12, 14:22-29, 26; 2 Chronicles 31; Nehemiah 10; and Amos 4:4.

The Sermon on the Amount

"SO YOU'RE SAYING Bill *bribed* you to come to the class?" I almost dropped my fork.

"Yeah, basically that's how it happened," Wayman pushed his steak and baked potato around on his plate.

"'I'll buy the nicest car on your lot,' he said, 'if you'll just come to three sessions.' Like I told you, I was willing to do anything for a sale…even go to a Bible class. I didn't know I was the one that would be taken for a ride. And what an amazing ride it's been!" Wayman stared through the restaurant wall for a moment. He looked more peaceful than I had ever seen him.

I finished chewing a bite. "So I'm supposed to ask you each week how you've been doing at letting go of your money and possessions, right?"

Wayman blinked and turned his focus back toward me. "Right. Yeah, well, let's see…I, uh…" He poked at his potato. "This isn't easy, you know? Talking about it. But I put a cheque in the church offering last Sunday for a fifth of all I made last month."

My eyes widened.

He leaned closer and said in a confidential tone, "I figure I got some catching up to do."

"Will your family get by okay?"

"Oh, yeah. I had a bunch of stuff I didn't need, and I hawked it."

"I noticed you're not wearing your nice ring and watch." I pointed at his hands.

"That's right. Back to the basics for me. Only what we need. Anyway, I put some of the money from the pawn shop into our chequing account for my wife to use for necessities. The rest I sent down to the rescue mission in town. Anonymously, you know. Don't want anyone making a big deal over it."

I shook my head. "That's amazing, Wayman. Good job."

"Well, God's been so good to me. It's a start." He took a bite of steak, then pushed his plate away. "So what about you, Joe? What can I be praying about for you?"

I had to think about that one for a moment. "Hmm. I guess I'm wrestling with how I'm supposed to apply this stuff we're learning in class. But I think my more immediate concern is, well…it's Jennifer. I'm starting to see that we have less and less in common, and I'm not sure what to do about it. I'd appreciate your prayers for wisdom."

"You got it, bro. Those woman problems can be real sticky. I know."

That's when the check arrived, which Wayman promptly snatched up. He paid the bill, and I must have said thank you at least five times.

We were walking out of the restaurant when Wayman suddenly stopped.

"Funny thing. Bill still hasn't told me what he's going to do with the car I sold him."

*   *   *

Jennifer was not happy.

"Bill," my girlfriend said in her businesslike manner, "today's passage is very harsh towards the rich. And all we ever seem to talk about is giving. I understand our topic is joyful generosity, but will we ever discuss other financial matters?"

The class had barely settled into our seats.

"Jennifer," Bill responded in an equally starched tone, "if you have a problem with this passage, I suggest you take up your grievance with the Author. As for our emphasis on giving, that also is a matter determined by God. He has chosen the emphasis throughout His Word because He knows that the most effective way for us to become free from materialism is by means of voluntary wealth-ectomy— that is, by giving. When we give, we grow…we change inside. In this way, giving affects our view of all other financial matters. So, the topic of giving is a natural starting point for any biblical discussion about wealth.

"Does that answer your question, Jennifer?"

Jennifer nodded reluctantly.

While we prayed for the class time, I watched Jennifer. She seemed resigned, maybe a little dejected. I reached over and put my hand on hers. She instantly jerked hers away. *Mood alert!* I made a mental note to proceed cautiously the rest of the day.

After prayer, Bill said, "Today's passage is not technically the Sermon on the…uh…Mount." He paused for our reaction. "Get it? Amount? Uh…mount?" Still no response.

"Well, anyway," he continued, undaunted, "The Sermon on the Mount is actually found in Matthew 5-7. Today's passage is from Luke's version of the sermon. Luke 6:17 describes the setting as **'a level place.'** So, this is a different location in which Jesus delivered a different sermon with some very similar content to the Sermon on the Mount. Perhaps we could call this the 'Sermon on the Green.'"

Bill laughed.

Only Bill laughed.

"You know...green grass. Green...money..." his voice trailed off.

What had we done to deserve such *pun*-ishment?

Someone had to put the group out of its misery, so I said, "I'll read today's passage."

Bill busied himself straightening his notes. "Fine, fine. Thank you, Joe."

"This is Luke 6:20-31," I said.

> [20]**Looking at his disciples, he said:**
>
> > **"Blessed are you who are poor,**
> > **for yours is the kingdom of God.**
> > [21]**Blessed are you who hunger now,**
> > **for you will be satisfied.**
> > **Blessed are you who weep now,**
> > **for you will laugh.**
> > [22]**Blessed are you when men hate you,**
> > **when they exclude you and insult you**
> > **and reject your name as evil, be-**
> > **cause of the Son of Man.**
>
> [23]**"Rejoice in that day and leap for joy,**
> **because great is your reward in heaven.**
> **For that is how their fathers treated the**
> **prophets.**
>
> > [24]**"But woe to you who are rich,**
> > **for you have already received your**
> > **comfort.**
> > [25]**Woe to you who are well fed now,**
> > **for you will go hungry.**
> > **Woe to you who laugh now,**
> > **for you will mourn and weep.**
> > [26]**Woe to you when all men speak well**
> > **of you,**

**for that is how their fathers
treated the false prophets.**

[27]**"But I tell you who hear me: Love your
enemies, do good to those who hate you,
[28]bless those who curse you, pray for
those who mistreat you.** [29]**If someone
strikes you on one cheek, turn to him the
other also. If someone takes your cloak,
do not stop him from taking your tunic.
[30]Give to everyone who asks you, and if
anyone takes what belongs to you, do not
demand it back.** [31]**Do to others as you
would have them do to you.**

Cathy read the passage again, and then she asked, "Is the first verse talking about people who are poor financially or poor spiritually, as in Matthew 5:3?"

"Both," Bill answered, "But for our discussion, we'll focus on the financially poor."

"The word 'poor' can be used other ways as well," I said. "I wouldn't want to miss some broader meaning by rushing to apply the verse only to money."

Bill bit his lip thoughtfully for a moment. "You have a point," he said. "In this sermon, Christ strongly teaches many expressions of love and grace for all lost and hurting people—even our enemies. But we can acknowledge the broader applicability while focusing in on one specific arena of application. And we should be careful not to *avoid* the implications for our financial lives, just because the passage also has other ramifications."

I nodded, and Bill shifted in his chair and continued, "In His sermon, Jesus first pronounced blessing upon the poor and the hungry. So tell me, why are the poor and hungry blessed?"

Samantha answered, "He says it's because the poor have the kingdom of God and the hungry will be satisfied."

Bill nodded. "Why them, though? Simply because they're poor and hungry?"

Jennifer frowned. "I'm not one to argue with God…," she looked pointedly at Bill, "but why should poverty or wealth make any difference in God's decision to bless?"

"Poor people have to trust God more," said Samantha. "Or at least they're more apt to."

Mrs. Coyne patted her granddaughter's knee. "That's right, dear. Poor people are used to being dependent on others." Then she dropped her eyes and said more quietly, "Sometimes too dependent." Then she looked up and continued, "So the poor have the advantage of being more ready to trust God, to look to Him in their need."

"So, Bill," said Wayman, "I suppose next you're going to ask why the rich get woe."

"That's right." Bill laughed. "I was coming to that."

In your own words, summarize Jesus' message for the poor. How does this affect you?

Wayman continued, "I'd say the young lady has pretty much answered that question too. Rich people put their faith where their money is, not in God."

"But there are many exceptions," Jennifer argued. "Surely there are rich people who will be blessed and poor people who will experience woe. Some rich people really do depend on God—Abraham and David, for instance. And some poor people don't trust God. Wouldn't it have been more accurate for Jesus to say, 'Blessed are those who rely on Me and woe to those who don't'?"

"That's not what Jesus said," said Cathy. "But I understand what you mean, Jennifer. I know I'm having a hard time hearing the harsh warnings in the Bible towards the rich. I'm tempted to ignore them by thinking that 'rich' only describes *other* people—not me."

"So, I suppose I should just quit my job and become poor." Jennifer spit the words. "Is that what I'm hearing?"

Bill assumed a mollifying tone. "Becoming economically poor is not necessarily a solution to the woes of wealth. Voluntary poverty can even be a form of prideful materialism, inviting a focus on self and on the material things one doesn't have rather than on God. Money and possessions are certainly good gifts from God, but we need to be acutely aware of the dangers of wealth."

"So it's not wrong to be rich?" I was searching for firm ground.

"I don't think so," Bill answered, "but don't ignore Jesus' warning. Being rich isn't wrong, but it is extremely dangerous."

Half to himself, Wayman muttered, "I'm sure glad we're saved by God's grace, not by what we've done."

Bill hesitated, then moved on. "In this passage, Jesus said, 'But woe to you who are rich, for you have already received your comfort—'"

In your own words, summarize Jesus' message for the rich. How does this affect you?

FYI: *Other warnings to the rich may be found in Psalm 49; Luke 16:19-31 (The Rich Man & Lazarus); Luke 18:24-25 (The Rich Ruler); and James 5:1-5 (a particularly harsh warning), as well as many other passages.*

"This doesn't seem like a fair trade," I blurted. "The rich get their comfort on earth, but in exchange God gives them *eternal* woe?"

"It doesn't seem fair, does it, Joe?" replied Bill. "But God doesn't force this trade on the rich. They choose it themselves. They bring on their own destruction."

Suddenly I felt very tired.

Mrs. Coyne said, "Bill, I think one of the reasons the rich will be punished is because they're the ones responsible for the world's poverty." She pointed a bony finger down at her opened Bible. "Right here, Proverbs 14:31 says, '**He who oppresses the poor shows contempt for their Maker.**' The rich exploit the poor to line their own pockets. They invest in oppressive and greedy global corporations, and they selfishly influence government legislation. The rich also—"

"That's ridiculous!" Jennifer interrupted. "The poor are responsible for their own mess, individually and collectively. They're lazy and won't pull their own weight." She flipped through her Bible as she spoke. "Proverbs 10:4 says, '**Lazy hands make a man poor, but diligent hands bring wealth.**'"

Are you satisfied with the level of comfort you have? If so, would you still be content if you were less comfortable?

What is the nature of the blessings and woes? When will they be experienced?

Mrs. Coyne raised her finger and started to speak. But whatever she said was drowned out as everyone simultaneously began to offer his or her opinion on the issue. Above the fray, I heard such phrases as "godless commies" and "Filthy money-grabbers."

A moment later, Bill was able to call us back to order, both arms raised for attention. "Stop! Everyone, just stop!"

He put one hand to his chest and panted for a few seconds. He looked pale. Then, regaining his composure, he said, "This is getting us nowhere. Blaming the poor or the rich is useless. That debate only divides Christians." He scanned around the room. I dropped my gaze.

Then he continued, "Look at Jesus' words in Luke 6:41-42, later in this same sermon:

> **Why do you look at the speck of sawdust in your brother's eye and pay no attention to the plank in your own eye? How can you say to your brother, 'Brother, let me take the speck out of your eye,' when you yourself fail to see the plank in your own eye? You hypocrite, first take the plank out of your eye, and then you will**

THE SERMON ON THE AMOUNT

see clearly to remove the speck from your brother's eye.

"Our first task is not to criticize others, but to examine our own hearts and be sure we're using God's money as He wishes. It's easy to ignore our responsibility by focusing on the behaviour of others."

"So, Bill," Wayman said quietly, "Are you now pointing out the specks in our eyes?" Startled, Bill looked at him, but then Wayman winked and grinned.

"Hey! I'm the one who gets to ask the questions around here," Bill said with a smile. "Although, I guess I have been known to express a strong opinion now and then."

He looked down at his Bible and gathered his thoughts. "Let's look at the rest of this passage now."

Jennifer jumped in. "I assume we're going to be focusing on the first part of verse 30, **'Give to everyone who asks you**.' But that's such a small part of the overall message. It's just one of many ways Jesus says we can express love."

"True," admitted Bill. "The passage is meant to be taken as a whole. Perhaps we should have read verses 32-38, because they are part of this section as well. But you're right, Jennifer, we will be focusing on verse 30. It's a particularly relevant statement in a Bible study on money and possessions. This verse also takes on extra significance in our society, which is so wealthy. Just so we don't miss the larger context, though, let's answer this question—what *is* Jesus' central message here?"

Cathy said, "God wants us to love Him and others in the same way God loves us. He's our example of extreme love. He didn't restrict Himself to 'fairness.' God loves us in ways that we simply do not deserve. He wants us to love that same way."

"Tough act to follow," grunted Wayman. "Seems to me if someone does something bad to me, I should get to do something bad back to him. Says here, '**If someone takes your cloak, do not stop him from taking your tunic**.' That sounds just plain stupid! One of our cars was stolen last month. So am I supposed to leave the gate open at night so they can take the rest?"

"I don't think…" Samantha hesitated. "I don't think we're supposed to just lay back and wait to get hurt. But we're supposed to do loving things for people who don't like us. Like God did for us."

"But that's not always practical." Cathy unconsciously placed protective hands over her growing tummy. "I don't think an abused wife should keep trying to take care of her husband if he keeps hitting her."

The group nodded in agreement.

"So, then," Bill said, "What do we do with Jesus' command, '**Give to everyone who asks you**'?"

"All I know is that I have to be careful when those homeless people harass me," declared Mrs. Coyne. "If I gave them money, they'd just waste it. I have no tolerance for waste."

Jennifer sat up straight in her chair. "Jesus did say, in Matthew 5:48—in the *real* Sermon on the Mount—'**Be perfect, therefore, as your heavenly Father is perfect**.' Whatever Jesus' command to give means—and I don't think we're to take it at face value—He wants us to obey it perfectly."

"How can we be perfect?" I asked. "We're sinful. Taking every word as a direct and literal command is legalism. The Pharisees turned God's Word into a set of rules and regulations, completely missing the point. As you said, Jenn, it's the overall message we need to pay attention to."

My girlfriend slowly raised her dreaded right eyebrow and glared at me frostily.

No doubt I'll hear about this later, I thought.

Bill broke in. "So, then, should we put qualifiers or conditions on Jesus' command?"

I responded first. "I think Jesus was exaggerating for effect."

"You're referring to a figure of speech called *hyperbole*," Bill offered.

I nodded enthusiastically. "Yeah, hyperbole. That doesn't mean we can ignore the command, but the command only makes sense if we don't take it literally."

"The verse does say to give," Cathy said, "but it doesn't say how much or in what form. When Bob and I don't make enough to give money, we make an extra effort to give of our time or our wisdom. Often these are even more valuable than money or possessions."

"And Bill," Mrs. Coyne added, "giving money may actually be harmful to poor people. Many of them have addictions. It's better to give money to a homeless shelter or buy a street person a sandwich."

How should we interpret Jesus' command, "Give to everyone who asks"?

"Now that you mention it," said Cathy, "I'm on the e-mail list for the downtown rescue mission. Just yesterday they sent out an announcement that someone had anonymously donated twenty thousand dollars!"

Is it wise to give freely to anyone who asks? Provide scriptural support for your answers, if possible.

I looked quickly at Wayman. He studiously examined his fingernails.

If you place any conditions or restrictions on Jesus' command to "give to everyone who asks," how can you guard against these becoming excuses for disobedience?

"You know," said Jennifer, "I really don't encounter a lot of poor people, maybe a panhandler now and then. Maybe this verse isn't as threatening as it first appears."

Mrs. Coyne responded with hot sarcasm, "Do you live in one of those gated communities, with security all around to keep out the riffraff? I ride the bus and walk around downtown and I get asked for money all the time. Avoiding the poor doesn't let anyone off the hook."

"Now, Sue." Bill held out a wrinkled hand. "Everyone here is working hard to apply this passage—Jennifer included. No one has it down pat."

How much contact do you have with the poor?

After an uncomfortable moment, Samantha said, "At least we know it's a good thing to give."

Bill smiled warmly. "Samantha, I couldn't have summarized the passage better myself." He turned to the group. "Folks, there are some tough teachings here and none of us can obey them perfectly. Fortunately, we're saved, not by satisfying this command, but by God's grace through Jesus Christ. His grace gives us greater and greater ability to obey His commands.

"But we cannot simply dismiss Jesus' hard sayings. Instead of coming up with reasons *not* to give, we should recognize all the good reasons *to* give. God's command is actually for our benefit. By giving we learn to rely, not on our wealth, but on His love and grace. And by giving, we receive blessings and eternal rewards that are far greater than the wealth we forfeit."

Bill looked at his watch. "In fact, that makes a good homework assignment. I want each of you to sit down and list all the reasons not to give to the poor and needy. Then list the reasons it's good to give.

"Next week's study is on worry, so we'll see you then."

Yeah, I thought, *if we're not overcome with worry by then!* The words of Jesus kept echoing in my mind, "**Woe to you who are rich. Woe to you who are rich. Woe…**"

A Brief Debrief

The three key points I took away from Jesus' Sermon on the "Green" were:

- As a wealthy person, I must beware the dangers of wealth.

- As I give generously, I will experience the blessings promised to the poor.

- I must be careful not to create loopholes so I can disobey Jesus' commands. By His grace, He will help me learn to live up to His high standards of obedience (though we'll never be perfect in this life—far from it).

If you thought the Old Testament Law was hard to fulfill, how do you think we can fulfill Jesus' command, "**Give to anyone who asks**"? The point in both Old and New Testaments is that we can't live the holy life by ourselves. We need God's grace and strength. With regard to our money, He will enable us to become increasingly generous and will build within us a heart that beats for His values. Rather than cowering away from the difficulty of obedience, take time frequently to talk to God about the heart He wants to create within you.

Is being rich a stumbling block for you in your faith?

List as many reasons as possible not to give to the poor and needy. Then list as many reasons as possible in favour of giving to the poor and needy.

Deeper Study

1. For further insights into Jesus' teaching, study the verses that follow this chapter's central passage (Luke 6:32-38), with particular attention to verse 38. Look

also at Matthew's parallel passages—Matthew 5:1-12 and 5:38-42.

2. Study John the Baptist's teaching in Luke 3:7-14. How is this similar to Jesus' teaching? How can we know if we have repented? How does John's teaching apply to us?

Two Treasuries, Two Masters

THE MOMENT HAD COME, but I still didn't know what to say. Jennifer sat across the small table, sipping her coffee and examining her nails. The Tuesday-night café crowd seemed far away as I searched for the words.

Jennifer...Jenn...Honey— No, not *honey.* Not at a time like this.

I wanted to be honest, but I didn't want to hurt her feelings. More than ever before, I understood what they mean when they say breaking up is hard to do. *It's harder for the break-er than for the break-ee,* I complained to myself. *I'm the one who has to do all the delicate work. God, help me to do this with your love for Jennifer.*

I was so intent on preparations that I didn't hear Jenn the first time she spoke.

"Joe, are you listening?"

I jumped to attention. "What? I'm sorry. What were you saying?"

"I said…" she sighed deeply, "I think we should end our relationship."

I was stunned.

She pursed her lips. "I'm not going to give you the standard 'it's-not-you-it's-me' speech. I think both of us have contributed to the problems in this relationship— especially when it comes to money. We just don't see eye-to-eye. I think we do make a strong couple, but I feel us diverging even more in our viewpoints as the money class goes on."

I finally found words, but not any that had crossed my mind before that moment. "Jenn, don't you think it goes even deeper?"

She continued as though she hadn't heard me. "You've started to treat giving as though it's this spiritual end-all. I mean, I'm glad you like the class, and I think we should be responsible with our money, but it's not wrong to have nice things."

"You're right, Jenn. I never said—"

"I sense condemnation from you. You seem critical of me because I don't want to give everything away and become a penniless nun."

"But that's not what I—"

"Joe, you haven't given everything away either, and God doesn't tell us all to give everything away. Your attitude seems a bit self-righteous."

"Self-righteous? How—"

"So I don't see any point in discussing it further. I trust we can be good friends, but I've decided we just aren't right for each other."

Her barrage was over and my meagre supply of verbal ammo was exhausted, so I surrendered without another word.

Not for the first time, we finished our coffee in silence.

Maybe I was wrong, I brooded. It's no party being the break-ee either.

*　　　*　　　*

The class felt different without Jennifer. I had seen her across the sanctuary during the worship service before the class, but she had apparently decided that she had better ways to use this hour. Her chair sat empty beside mine.

After giving his latest excuse for not having yet brought baked goods to class, Bill shifted the focus off himself. "Sue, would you please read today's passage? It's Matthew 6:19-24."

"All right, Bill," Mrs. Coyne replied. She adjusted her glasses and peered down at her Bible.

> [19]**"Do not store up for yourselves treasures on earth, where moth and rust destroy, and where thieves break in and steal. [20]But store up for yourselves treasures in heaven, where moth and rust do not destroy, and where thieves do not break in and steal. [21]For where your treasure is, there your heart will be also.**
>
> [22]**"The eye is the lamp of the body. If your eyes are good, your whole body will be full of light. [23]But if your eyes are bad, your whole body will be full of darkness. If then the light within you is darkness, how great is that darkness!**
>
> [24]**"No one can serve two masters. Either he will hate the one and love the other, or he will be devoted to the one and despise the other. You cannot serve both God and Money."**

Wayman read the passage again for us. Then Bill looked around the circle, skipping self-consciously past Jennifer's chair. "Now, we already briefly discussed verse 21, about our treasures and our hearts. However, that was way back in our first meeting, and quite a bit of water has passed under our respective bridges since then. So let's take another look at those statements first. Why did Jesus say we shouldn't store up treasures for ourselves on earth?"

Cathy started hesitantly, "I'm not sure I'm really ready to swallow this pill...but it seems that we should do it just because God commands it, plain and simple. We need to obey God because He is God. There shouldn't have to be any other reasons."

"Yeah, I'm sure that's true," Samantha said, "but I think there are many more reasons for storing our treasure in heaven. Jesus says stuff down here can be destroyed or it can wear out. My car has a few rust spots, and I found two of my son's old sweaters moth-eaten just last month."

"And thieves!" Mrs. Coyne wagged her knobby index finger. "Criminals often take advantage of us senior citizens. If you ask me, the banks and the government are the worst thieves of all! Every month my pension money is eaten away by service fees, inflation, taxes—and they told me my money would be safe."

"It's interesting you use the phrase *eaten away,* Sue," Bill said. "The word for *rust* in this passage means literally 'an eating.' Jesus painted a word picture of material wealth as something that is easily devoured."

Wayman scratched his thin beard. "You know, next to my car lot there's a huge storage facility. Huge. You can rent space to keep extra furniture...boxes...whatever. Sometimes people keep their things there for years. Not only does the stuff sit unused—it costs money *not* to use it! These sayings of Jesus made me think about that storage place. You know, it seems like it would be better not to get any of that stuff—or to get rid of it—than to just keep it sitting around like that. And you can't lose what you don't have, right?"

"But that doesn't mean it's wrong to save money, does it?" Cathy objected. "It's foolish not to plan for the future." She looked down and patted her swollen belly. "Especially when so much is riding on it."

"Absolutely right, Cathy," answered Bill. "Proverbs has several verses praising the wisdom of saving, and we will have an in-depth discussion on that very topic in a couple of weeks, when we study the Parable of the Rich Fool."

I interjected a question, "What does Jesus mean by *treasures,* though? Is He referring only to money and goods, or also to intangibles like relationships?"

"That's a wonderful point," Cathy agreed. "I consider my family my greatest treasure!"

Bill smiled and pondered for a moment. "In the Greek, the word for *treasures* means 'deposits' or 'stores one lays up.' Figuratively, I guess, treasures might be anything of value. It's possible Jesus is referring to different types of treasures on earth and in heaven. But since He talks about physical destruction, He's pretty clearly intending earthly treasures to mean money and possessions."

"Huh," Wayman grunted loudly, bent over and intently examining his open Bible. "Seems like the big difference isn't the kind of treasure, but the place it's kept. Maybe there's a way to keep the same kind of treasure—you know, like money—in heaven." He raised his puzzled face to the group.

"Well, sure," answered Samantha. "Where it's stored makes all the difference in the world. Anything we keep down here will be useless sooner or later. But something kept in heaven will be there forever." For the first time I could remember, she looked us each in the eye as she spoke. "That's a big difference!"

"So we're not just talking about two treasures, but two treasuries," Bill suggested.

YOUR MONEY OR YOUR LIFE

"Yeah," Samantha continued enthusiastically. "My friends, and the commercials on TV—they all say that having more things is what's important. But all the people I know who have lots of money and lots of stuff—they're all so stressed and busy. I don't think their lives are any better than mine." She looked down. "I guess real life is only with Jesus. The only important thing is how we stand with God."

Bill nodded solemnly. "And with that apt word, let's shift our focus upward. Why *should* we store up treasures in *heaven*?"

How are earthly treasures and heavenly treasures different?

What does it mean to **"store up for yourselves treasures on earth"?**

A thoughtful silence followed. I reread the verse to myself, "**But store up for yourselves treasures in heaven**." Then I voiced a sudden thought, "Hey, it says *for yourselves*. At first, I thought storing any kind of treasure for myself was selfish. But Jesus urges us to store up treasures in heaven *for ourselves*. That's an answer to your question, then, Bill. We should store up treasures in heaven because then we get to enjoy them for all eternity."

"Very good observation," said Bill. "It's not wrong or selfish to want for ourselves the very same things that God wants us to have, and that includes treasure in heaven. It's actually a very godly and mature desire."

Wayman responded in a low voice, "If only treasure on earth wasn't so much fun."

"Another reason to store up treasure in heaven is just what Cathy said," Mrs. Coyne pointed out. "Just because our Lord commands us to. We don't really need any other reasons, I don't think."

"I agree, Grandma, we don't," Samantha said. "But the thing that stuck with me from that very first class is that our heart follows our treasure. Jesus said right here, in verse 21, '**For where your treasure is, there your heart will be**

also.' So it's good to store up treasure in heaven because then we can be sure that our heart will be in heaven too."

More forcefully than I intended, I responded, "But our hearts have to be right before we will do the right things, Samantha."

Samantha's cheeks flushed and she looked down at her Bible for a moment. But then she looked at me and said gently, in a slightly quaking voice, "Maybe you're right. But that's not what I think Jesus is saying here. Sometimes we just have to make decisions about where we put our treasure, and then our hearts will end up in the same place."

She glanced at her grandmother, then lowered her head, pushing her glasses back with one finger. Mrs. Coyne reached over and patted Samantha's hand.

Wayman sat chewing his lip, then said, somewhat reluctantly, "I think I know what she…what Samantha means. A while back, I sold a van to a homeless shelter. They couldn't afford much, so I pawned a worthless vehicle off on them." He stared out the classroom window. "The van lasted three months, which was a miracle. Well, then I felt bad and decided to give them a better van as a replacement." His gaze sharpened and took in the circle of people. "Just good for repeat business, you know."

A couple of heads nodded.

Wayman continued, "I took the second van over myself, and the shelter director gave me a tour and explained what they do." He dropped his gaze. "I guess I never really knew until then how difficult some of their lives are. Now, I've worked hard

What does it mean to "store up for yourselves treasures in heaven"?

How can we enjoy God's material blessings without storing up treasures for ourselves on earth?

every day of my life, and I can't stand lazy people. Some of those homeless people need to pull up their socks and get their lives together. However, some are sick and have real bad addictions. Some of them even have kids. I saw their faces. And God did something inside me."

He stopped and rubbed his eyes. "Anyway, I guess I'm saying that I put a little bit of my treasure in that homeless shelter, and then my heart changed."

Silence. The faint cry of a baby wafted down the hall from the church nursery, and somewhere outside a dog barked.

I might be the only one here who knows that just happened two days ago, I mused to myself.

Finally, gently, Cathy said, "Wayman, if I didn't know better, I'd say you're a different man than you were when this class began." Her eyes twinkled.

Wayman glanced at her, then back at his hands. "Don't know what you're talking about," he said gruffly, shifting uncomfortably in his seat.

Bill rescued him from further embarrassment. "Thank you, Wayman, for sharing such a valuable life lesson." He glanced at his watch. "Unfortunately, folks, due to time constraints, we will have to skip a formal discussion of verses 22 and 23. Let's look at verse 24 now. '**No one can serve two masters**.' Why not?"

"I know that slavery was common in Jesus' day," I said.

FYI*: Verses 22-23 are difficult to interpret. However, from the context, they seem to relate to one's heart attitude toward money and God. The eyes are the inward gateway by which light and sight enter the body. The eyes are also very expressive and can be an outward gateway, revealing attitudes of the heart. Jesus may have had either or both of these meanings in mind. Our value system can clarify or cloud the way we perceive worldly wealth and God. A look of contentment can reveal the light of godly insight, and a look of turmoil can bring up the darkness of materialism within our hearts.*

"And while it's hard for us to identify with that practice, in that day slavery meant the commitment of one's whole self—your whole life. Of course, each person only has one self to give, so it was impossible to serve as a slave to two different masters."

"Yeah," Cathy agreed. "Nowadays lots of people work two jobs and have two bosses, but we only have to commit a certain part of our week to each one. A better illustration today would be a man who tries to keep up with two wives. A bigamist can't give two different women the care and attention he can give to just one."

Bill suddenly sobered. "I know my friend Ron tried to keep both his wife and his mistress happy for a while." He swallowed hard. "It was impossible."

"Says here, '**You cannot serve both God and Money**,'" Wayman quoted. "Reminds me of that sermon from a couple weeks go. About the golden calf.

In your experience, why is it impossible to serve both God and Money?

Remember how the people of Israel worshiped that…that idol made out of their jewellery. But I don't see people serving or worshiping money like that any more."

"What, are you blind?" Mrs. Coyne's index finger rose again. "I know a lot of people who are beholden to money. There are plenty of rich people who show off their gigantic houses and parade their fancy cars and clothes. If that's not worshiping money, I don't know what is." She cast a nervous glance toward Jennifer's chair.

"And what about debt?" Cathy added. "I see a lot of people weighed down by debt to credit cards, to department stores,

FYI: The word translated Money in verse 24 is a values-neutral term meaning "wealth" or "property" (as opposed to the English "mammon" in some translations, which inaccurately connotes unrighteous wealth). Money is not evil in itself, but we can make it an idol that takes God's place.

to banks. Bob and I would never want to put our family in that predicament. Too many people are forced to service their debt instead of serving God. Proverbs 22:7 says, '**The borrower is servant to the lender**.' Unfortunately, we've recently had difficulty paying off our credit card each month."

Samantha looked worried. "Debt is scary. I mean, I know how much God wants to be worshiped and how mad He gets when we worship anything else. But money can be so sneaky, and we can be attached to it without even knowing."

How does God feel, and what does He think, when we serve Money as our master? (How is it similar to marital infidelity?)

Bill responded kindly, "Indeed, many of us do serve money, and being in debt can be a sign that we are attached to our things. If we serve money, we don't blatantly call our possessions 'gods,' as the Israelites called the calf, but that's what they are. We think the Israelites' sin is obvious, but it wasn't so obvious to them. Even Moses' brother Aaron, the high priest, joined in! We don't think we worship our wealth, but ask people in other countries what they think of our attitude. I believe many of our Christian leaders are beholden to wealth just as Aaron was. If that's true, it doesn't bode well for the people they're leading, does it?

"Let's put our money in God's heavenly bank, where it will earn the highest interest rate available and our deposits are guaranteed for all eternity!

"Wealth isn't evil in and of itself. But when we devote to money the first and best of our time, the first and best of our energy, the first and best of our heart affections—then we're putting it in God's place. Do you work primarily for money? Or do you earn money in order to serve God? Which do you think of first in the morning—God or money? Around which master do you plan your life?"

Bill allowed this to sink in. Then he dismissed us a few minutes early. He suddenly seemed unusually tired.

It was strange to walk out of the classroom alone.

A Brief Debrief

The four key points I gleaned from that particular class come straight from Jesus' teaching:

- **"Do not store up for yourselves treasures on earth."** These *treasures* include at least our money and possessions. We are not prohibited from saving money or buying nice things, but all of these decisions must be for God's purposes.

- **"Store up for yourselves treasures in heaven."** Giving freely and spending wisely, according to God's will, is a better investment than any stock on the earthly market, because it buys treasure that can never be lost—treasure that will pay interest forever.

- **"Where your treasure is, there your heart will be also."** If you don't feel like giving generously of your money—or your time—simply make the decision to do it and God will see that the enthusiasm follows.

- **"You cannot serve both God and Money."** While none of us is perfect in our devotion to God, if we are predominantly devoted to money or to anything else, then God is not our Master.

Examine your life. Where is your treasure? Where, then, is your heart? Who is your master?

By God's grace, anyone can come to a point where he or she can answer, "My treasure and heart are in heaven, and God is my Master." No matter what your history, you can start a new commitment to God today. If you've been "married" to money, this is one instance where "divorce" is permitted, and there is no waiting period for it to take effect.

Do you generally store up treasures on earth or in heaven?

What obstacles sometimes prevent you from storing up treasures in heaven?

Deeper Study

Use one or more commentaries to learn how Jesus and Matthew may have meant Matthew 6:22-23 to fit into this context, and how these statements may relate to those preceding and following them.

Don't Worry,
Be . . . Joyful!

JENNIFER WAS BACK. Not back in my life, but back in the class. When I walked into the classroom, I was surprised to see her sitting primly next to Bill's accustomed seat. I took a chair across the circle from her, and she gave me a matter-of-fact "Hi, Joe," and continued chatting with Cathy as though she had never been gone.

Bill arrived, wincing more than usual as he walked with his cane. Once again, all seven class members were present. Frankly, I was amazed at the consistent attendance.

We prayed, then Bill said, "Gang, today's passage starts right where we left off last week in Matthew It's Jesus' teaching about worry in the Sermon on the Mount. Cathy, would you please read Matthew 6:25-34 for us?"

Cathy nodded and read:

> **[25]"Therefore I tell you, do not worry about your life, what you will eat or drink; or about your body, what you will wear. Is not life more important than food, and the body more important than**

clothes? [26]Look at the birds of the air;
they do not sow or reap or store away in
barns, and yet your heavenly Father feeds
them. Are you not much more valuable
than they? [27]Who of you by worrying can
add a single hour to his life?
   [28]"And why do you worry about
clothes? See how the lilies of the field
grow. They do not labor or spin. [29]Yet I
tell you that not even Solomon in all his
splendor was dressed like one of these.
[30]If that is how God clothes the grass of
the field, which is here today and tomorrow is thrown into the fire, will he not
much more clothe you, O you of little
faith? [31]So do not worry, saying, 'What
shall we eat?' or 'What shall we drink?'
or 'What shall we wear?' [32]For the pagans run after all these things, and your
heavenly Father knows that you need
them. [33]But seek first his kingdom and his
righteousness, and all these things will be
given to you as well. [34]Therefore do not
worry about tomorrow, for tomorrow will
worry about itself. Each day has enough
trouble of its own."

After we read the section again, Bill said, "So, according to
this passage, why shouldn't we worry?"

Jennifer was quick to respond, "Reverend Moss says
that whenever we see the word *therefore,* we need to ask
ourselves what it's there for. Here it provides a logical link
with the verses we studied last week."

I frowned. The verses "we" studied? She wasn't even
here.

But if Jennifer saw my reaction, she ignored it. "In the last passage, Jesus finished by saying, 'You cannot serve both God and Money.' Now He continues, 'Therefore I tell you, do not worry about your life, what you will eat or drink; or about your body, what you will wear.' He's saying that if we're worrying about our finances, we're serving money—we're trusting in riches instead of God."

"When you have a young family, it's hard *not* to worry about food or clothes or other necessities," said Cathy. "Sometimes the only reason I try to stop worrying is just because Jesus commanded me not to."

According to Matthew 6:25-34, why shouldn't we worry? (List as many reasons as you can.)

Samantha looked up from her Bible. "I think Jesus explains part of the reason not to worry when He says, '**Is not life more important than food, and the body more important than clothes?**'"

I decided to play devil's advocate: "But we could starve or die of hypothermia without enough food or clothes."

Samantha giggled. "He's not saying you shouldn't have any. He's only saying that there's more to life than those things."

Amazing! I chuckled to myself. A woman who doesn't think clothes are the most important thing in life!

"Reminds me of a verse I just learned," said Wayman. He cleared his throat. "'**Cast all your anxiety on him because he cares for you.**' I think it's 1 Peter 5:7. It says God's going to take good care of us."

"And another passage," added Bill, "which goes along with Jesus' talk about caring for the birds, is Matthew 10:29-31, '**Are not two sparrows sold for a penny? Yet not one of them will fall to the ground apart from the will of your Father. And even the very hairs of your head are all numbered. So don't be afraid; you are worth more than many sparrows.**' And back here in Matthew 6, He made the same point about the lilies. Jesus is using the classic argument from the lesser to the greater. If He cares so well for birds and flowers, how much more will He provide for us?"

"So when it comes to choosing a master," I reasoned, "we'd be hard pressed to choose one who cares more about our interests than God does. Sounds like being God's slave is the best kind of freedom."

"Great insight," said Bill. "Try getting that kind of love and caring from money or possessions as your master."

I took the matter one step further. "So, essentially, worry is believing God doesn't love us and won't take care of us."

Bill nodded enthusiastically.

Samantha absently tapped her nose with her pen. "When Jesus says that the birds don't sow or reap or store food in barns, and the lilies don't labour or spin, it almost sounds like God will give us everything we need, no matter what, even if we do nothing."

"No way, no how!" The force of Jennifer's objection took us all aback. "Proverbs says laziness will lead to poverty. God doesn't want us frittering away our time or money. Even the birds have to work to find food. The flowers have to process soil nutrients. We shouldn't worry, but life is not a free ride."

FYI: *Proverbs 10:4; 12:24, 27; 19:15; 26:15 all talk about laziness.*

Samantha shrugged. "Maybe some people make too big a deal about work."

Jennifer's face reddened. "I have a right to be proud of my work ethic. There's nothing wrong with that."

Samantha's eyes widened. "I'm sorry, I didn't mean to say anything bad about your work. I just thought that since the flowers and birds don't have any cares, then—"

"Having no cares sounds careless," Jennifer interrupted. "God gave us our things so that we would steward them wisely. So are we just supposed to ignore vandals and thieves? In fact—"

"Now, now, ladies." Bill stepped in. "Each of you has a good point. On the one hand, it's good to take care of God's wealth. On the other hand, we are often far too concerned with protecting our property. Worry is so common that many people now think it's imprudent *not* to worry!

"Take this church building, for example. Certainly, we should clean and maintain it, but we shouldn't get all upset when a youth activity causes a little damage. God's property is for ministry—and that goes for the property He's placed in your care." Bill rubbed one of his bony knuckles.

As I scanned the passage, I noticed yet another reason not to worry. "In verse 27, Jesus asks whether worrying can add even a single hour to our lives. Of course, it can't. In fact, medical science has discovered that stress and anxiety cause all kinds of illnesses and sometimes shorten our life span."

"And—" Mrs. Coyne poked at the page, "I notice that Jesus made a clear distinction between Christians and pagans in verse 32. If non-Christians worry, then we should do just the opposite."

"Christians do have good reason to trust in God," Bill agreed. "Unfortunately, however, we are not always so different from pagans in practice. In fact, anxiety in our culture exceeds that of any other culture or time." He punctuated the last several words by pounding his cane on the floor. He continued, gesticulating broadly, "We...we waste so much time and effort urgently making money so...so we can buy products and services—*things that nobody even heard of thirty years ago*—"

Suddenly Bill stopped. He slowly lowered his arms and grinned sheepishly. "Guess I got carried away there. It's...it's just that I remember clearly how my friend Ron got so caught up in trusting money. He was one of the hardest workers I've ever known, but he was replacing faith in God with faith in his own productivity, and that was part of what led to his many griefs."

Bill paused to examine his notes. "Where were we? Oh, yes. Any more reasons why we shouldn't worry?"

After a moment's silence, Samantha answered, "I think verse 33 is pretty important: '**But seek first his kingdom and his righteousness, and all these things will be given to you as well.**' It's kind of like the way you can't serve two masters. You can't worry about money and seek God's kingdom at the same time."

"And if we do seek His kingdom," added Cathy, "Jesus promises to supply us with all the necessities as a matter of course. No need to worry."

Mrs. Coyne turned to a bookmarked page in her Bible. "One of my favourite passages on worry is Philippians 4:6-7: 'Do **not be anxious about anything, but in everything, by prayer and petition, with thanksgiving, present your requests to God. And the peace of God, which tran-scends all understanding, will guard your hearts and your minds in Christ Jesus.**' When we take our needs to God, we're relying on Him instead of money." She smiled and looked down. "Of course, even though I pray, I sometimes have a hard time believing the promise later in that same chapter, in verse 19: '**And my God will meet all your needs ac-cording to his glorious riches in Christ Jesus.**'"

Bill turned toward her. "That's one of my favourite passages too, Sue."

Why do some of us worry, knowing that we live in the wealthiest society in human history?

Why do we worry when we have God as our Provider?

How can we stop worrying?

Mrs. Coyne thought for a moment. "One of my prob-lems, though, is telling the difference between what I need and what I don't need. How many outfits do I need? Should I stock food ahead of time or only buy what I can eat at the time? Should I get my hair done, so I'll fit in with my friends and co-workers, or should I let it go?"

Everybody nodded in agreement, and I began to mentally review the "needs" on which I had spent money during the previous week.

"Well," said Wayman, "I don't know how much this helps, but I always used to think I needed at least as much as I had the day before. If something broke or got old, I said I needed a new one." He shook his head. "But I guess I really meant I just needed to get back to where I was before. And the more money I had, the more things I thought I needed."

"It's a lot easier to raise our standard of living than to lower it," I agreed. "I can't imagine getting by now on what I had in college."

"It's those advertisers that are to blame!" Mrs. Coyne wagged her finger. "They practically hypnotize us. I have half a mind to throw my TV out the window. **'What good will it be for a man if he gains the whole world, yet forfeits his soul?'**[*]

"What about you, Bill?" I asked impulsively. "How many shirts do you have? When do you go and get a new car? What do you consider a need?"

Bill smiled and nodded slowly. "That's a good question...one we should ask ourselves regularly. Such a habit can help us be more grateful for what we have.

Do you worry about food, clothing or shelter? If so, how much more money do you need in order to stop worrying about these things?

List some examples of true needs and true wants in your life.

"But we're running a bit short on time and I want to ask another question that goes with that one: How much can I give? This question turns our perspective away from our-

[*] Matthew 16:26.

selves. Instead of moaning about what we don't have, we think about what others need. We think about God's work. When we ask, 'What do I need?' we tend to worry and think selfishly. Sometimes we're like little children greedily clutching our candy as it melts in our hands and drips onto the ground.

"But asking, *What can I give?* is like holding our hands open to God and to others. It shows love, and our hearts will almost always follow our gifts. When we give, we grant God greater access to our hearts, and our hands are open to receive His eternal blessings."

Bill paused, then continued, "In the last verse of Matthew 6, Jesus says, '**Do not worry about tomorrow, for tomorrow will worry about itself.**' Now—"

Jennifer broke in. "We can certainly save for tomorrow, though, Bill, even if we don't have to worry about it."

"I agree, Jennifer," Bill said. "That verse definitely doesn't say we shouldn't be prepared. It's utter foolishness and a waste of God's resources when we don't plan ahead. We'll get back to that next week."

Jennifer turned to her class outline in her carefully organized notebook and nodded. She then glanced at me and rolled her eyes, as if to say, *Finally, we're coming to something practical.*

"However," Bill continued, "the Bible calls us to a radically different mindset than the one most of us have. We should save responsibly, but we should never rely on our savings."

Jennifer gave a hesitant nod.

"Now," said Bill, "I have one last and most important question. It's at the centre of every Christian's faith. Jesus says we are to seek God's kingdom and His righteousness, rather than worry about things—even about necessities. But what does that mean in practice? *How do we seek the kingdom?*"

We all looked at each other for several seconds.

Then Cathy flipped back a page in her Bible. "The Lord's Prayer is earlier in this same chapter—in Matthew 6:9-13. I read it this week, and noticed that the first three things Christ tells us to pray for are God's name to be hallowed or revered, God's kingdom to come, and God's will to be done. After all this, *then* Jesus tells us to ask for our daily bread. So maybe those first three requests show us something about how to seek God's kingdom, at least in prayer."

"Excellent observation, Cathy," said Bill. "So what do those pursuits look like in our daily lives?"

Still more silence.

Finally, Bill turned toward Wayman, who was studiously avoiding eye contact with anyone else. "Wayman, I believe you told me you would be willing to share with the group about the way God has been working in your life these last few weeks. Your story would be a very appropriate answer to this question."

Wayman glanced at Bill, then around the group. "Yeah, well, I guess I've been holding out on most of you," he said, overly loud.

Lord, help him not be too nervous, I prayed.

Immediately Wayman breathed a huge sigh and relaxed visibly. "Back when we studied Zacchaeus, that was when God got hold of me. He showed me that I was serving and worshiping money, not God. Like Jesus says here, '**For the pagans run after all these things**.' That was me."

As he spoke, Wayman's confidence grew. I could hear the salesman coming out, only now he was selling truth and life. Optimism replaced his former arrogance, and I heard passion for God, not for money.

He continued, "But I wasn't happy at all. The more I had, the more I worried. What if I lost my business? What if my house got robbed? What if, what if, what if... Now God's helping me to stop worrying and to go after the things of His kingdom. I still want to work hard, but I want to do it for God."

Cathy smiled, and Mrs. Coyne's knowing nod said, *I suspected as much.*

"A few weeks ago, when I realized how concerned I was with money and things, I decided to give away a chunk of income. It was the only way to get free. And since then, I've felt a lot better. Peaceful." He chuckled. "Yeah, joyful.

"I loaned out some of my stuff too, like one of my extra cars to a neighbour lady. I'm also going through everything and getting rid of things I haven't used in a while. I don't want to worry about any of it any more. It all gets so heavy, like chains around my neck."

I noticed Jennifer shifting in her chair, a frown growing between her carefully groomed eyebrows.

"We still lock our doors, but I cancelled the security alarm. I don't have as much stuff to protect anymore, see? The amount I was paying to the alarm company every month—now I'm giving it to the church. On top of my regular giving, that is."

Practically speaking, how do we seek first God's kingdom and His righteousness?

Jennifer burst out, "But Wayman, you have a family. You should be careful to keep enough for their security, to provide for their needs."

Wayman chuckled again and looked directly at Jennifer. "That's the excuse I used for years to keep on living just like these pagans Jesus talks about. I would put a little money in the church offerings, just to feel good. But I really wasn't living any different than my non-Christian friends." He finished softly, "I decided it was time for me to live for the kingdom of God."

No one spoke for a long moment. Jennifer's manicured nails tapped on her notebook cover.

I wondered to myself, *Why don't I have a story to share about the way I've changed?*

Then Cathy said quietly, "Thank you for sharing, Wayman. I needed to hear that."

Mrs. Coyne sounded nervous as she said, "I have two locks and a chain on each of my doors. And I have a small annuity set aside. Am I too worried? How much security is enough?"

Bill answered, "No security on earth is enough. Nothing of this world can save us from every threat. That's why Jesus instructed us to put our security in heaven...in God. When we look to earthly resources for security, the answer to 'How much?' is, 'Just a little bit more'. Just one more deadbolt. Just a bit more money. It's never enough, because we are never completely safe down here. Our material goods are never totally safe.

"We worry *because* we're so wealthy. We easily forget Almighty God's security plan—to seek first His kingdom and His righteousness, with the assurance all our physical needs will be provided as well.

"And let's be very careful about covertly trusting money in the name of 'stewardship.' When you guard your possessions, don't guard them so tightly that you don't hear God when He tells you to let go."

Bill glanced at his watch. "I'm sorry, we've run a couple minutes over. During the week, think about this homework question: How can I use my money to seek God's kingdom?"

I jotted down the question on a card to put on my fridge. I vowed to display it even more prominently than the pizza fliers.

The group began to disperse. "Oh, I almost forgot!" Bill exclaimed. "We will have a guest next week. Most of you probably know Steve Malone. He's a financial planner who serves on our church's board of directors. Steve will participate in our discussion on saving and storing as we study the Parable of the Rich Fool."

Jennifer strode briskly by me on her way out, eyes on the floor, muttering under her breath, "About time we got someone in here with some sense."

I meant to ask her how she was doing, but before I could catch her, she was gone.

A Brief Debrief

The two key points I learned from that class session are really flip sides of the same truth:

- Do not worry.

- Trust God to provide your needs.

If worry were a disease, it would be considered an epidemic in our society, even within our churches. Parents worry about providing enough for their families. College students worry about their careers. Older people worry about retirement. Maybe we worry so much because we have so much to lose.

God is our faithful Protector and Provider. He takes care of the birds and the flowers, so of course He will take care of us. This doesn't mean we can be lazy or careless with the resources God gives us. We should work hard, pray for His guidance, and act wisely with finances. Above all, we should have no doubt that God will provide.

What is most likely to cause you anxiety? What does this say about your view of God?

Deeper Study

1. Study in greater depth these Bible passages on worry: Matthew 10:26-31; Philippians 4:6-7, 19; 1 Peter 5:7. Take time also to examine any other passages that you find personally comforting.

2. Compare Luke 12:22-31 with Matthew 6:25-34. These parallel passages are almost exactly the same. Does Luke intend any different emphasis from this passage in the context of his book? Do the small differences between the two passages open any new insights on the topic of worry and our handling of money?

The Rich Fool: A Soul-Searching Opportunity

"HELLO, EVERYONE. MY NAME is Steve." From his seat beside Bill, the visitor glanced around the circle of faces. "My true identity is church board treasurer, but by day I don the guise of a mild-mannered financial planner here in town."

The group smiled. Jennifer's gaze verged on adoration.

"I'm grateful to Bill for asking me to come and participate in your study of the parable of the rich fool. I've heard that this group has some great discussions about money in the Bible. As you can imagine, I believe this is a critical topic, and I always want to grow in my own understanding." Suddenly his features sagged in mock sorrow. "However, the real reason I came is that I expected to find some of Bill's famous baked goods waiting here."

Bill feigned anxiety as he put a hand on Steve's shoulder. "You're not leaving us, are you?" When Steve gave an exaggerated noncommittal shrug, Bill smiled and continued, "Well, leave if you must, but as long as you can stand to be with us, please make yourself at home and feel free to share from your expertise."

Steve nodded and smiled back.

Bill opened his Bible. "As you mentioned, we're looking at the rich fool today. In fact, Steve, if you wouldn't mind reading the passage aloud..."

Steve agreed and read Luke 12:13-21:

[13]**Someone in the crowd said to him, "Teacher, tell my brother to divide the inheritance with me."** [14]**Jesus replied, "Man, who appointed me a judge or an arbiter between you?"** [15]**Then he said to them, "Watch out! Be on your guard against all kinds of greed; a man's life does not consist in the abundance of his possessions."** [16]**And he told them this parable: "The ground of a certain rich man produced a good crop.** [17]**He thought to himself, 'What shall I do? I have no place to store my crops.'** [18]**"Then he said, 'This is what I'll do. I will tear down my barns and build bigger ones, and there I will store all my grain and my goods.** [19]**And I'll say to myself, "You have plenty of good things laid up for many years. Take life easy; eat, drink and be merry."'** [20]**"But God said to him, 'You fool! This very night your life will be demanded from you. Then who will get what you have prepared for yourself?'**

[21]"This is how it will be with anyone who stores up things for himself but is not rich toward God."

After we read the passage a second time, Bill began, "In the first verse of this section, the man in the crowd wanted our Lord to act as an inheritance arbitrator between him and his brother. Why didn't Jesus settle this dispute?"

Parables are sometimes difficult to understand, but the context usually provides clues as to a parable's main point. To whom did Jesus address this parable? How did Jesus summarize the parable?

"The man seems to be trying to manipulate Jesus," said Mrs. Coyne. "Rather than inviting Jesus to mediate impartially, he audaciously told Jesus what to do."

Jennifer turned to Steve. "But wouldn't people naturally look to Him to answer questions like this?"

Steve cleared his throat. "It's true that priests and teachers of the day were responsible for settling civil lawsuits and controversies. As a recognized teacher or *rabbi*, Jesus could easily have intervened here. Why didn't He? Perhaps Jesus wanted to distinguish Himself from the Pharisees and teachers of the Law, who would've handed down a cut-and-dried decision one way or the other. It's also possible Jesus didn't want to get mired down as an arbitrator; that wasn't His mission."

Cathy said, "I think Jesus divinely sensed that this man's motives weren't right. He was greedy. So, instead of ruling in this case, Christ responded with the rich fool parable."

"The man may have had a legitimate complaint," said Bill, "but that's irrelevant. Love for his brother should have led him to sacrifice some of his rights, but as Cathy said, his greed got in the way of love. Rather than getting involved in petty divisiveness, Jesus went to the root of the matter by warning the man against greed."

"Yeah," said Wayman, "and Jesus meant this parable for us too. We—"

"What?" Jennifer broke in. "You mean to compare us with this guy? Sure, we're all occasionally a little selfish, Wayman, but I don't think Jesus would feel the need to tell *us* the parable of the rich fool."

Wayman thought for a moment, then ran his finger down the page of his open Bible. "Well, when Jesus gave the parable, He taught it to everyone there. See, in verses 15 and 16? I don't know about you, but I know I sure need to listen to what Jesus said."

"Me too," said a soft voice. We all turned to Samantha, who continued, "None of us wanted to think we were like the rich ruler, but we are. I'm a selfish fool, too, at times. I think we all are."

"Speak for yourself, *Samantha*." I shivered as Jennifer spoke. "The rich fool is clearly so godless that we can hardly be compared to him."

Bill broke in, "Why don't we move on and discuss the parable itself, then? Let's go through it carefully, asking this question: *What did the rich fool do wrong?*"

Wayman said loudly, "Sounds good to me, Bill. This guy here—must have been a farmer—he had a good year. But in this passage, he says 'I' six times and 'my' four times. He doesn't once say anything about God. But God's the one who made the land and grew those crops, not the farmer!"

"That's right," said Steve. "We must listen to God when we're making major financial decisions."

"What if we don't hear anything?" I asked.

Steve replied, "Then use the good sense God gave you, Joe."

"But God's will often doesn't make sense to us," I responded, confused. "Jesus' command to the rich young ruler to give everything away seems foolish and short-sighted. Our Lord highly praised Zacchaeus's bizarre and extreme actions. On the other hand, it makes good common sense to increase your savings when your income increases. That's what the rich fool decided to do. If you have a bumper crop, it doesn't seem foolish to put some of it away for the future."

The room was silent.

After a moment, Bill said, "Joe, you have some valid observations. But let's see how the fool completed his plan in verse 19: '**And I'll say to myself,** *How much do you pray about financial decisions? If you consult God, but don't hear anything, what do you do?*

19: '**And I'll say to myself, "You have plenty of good things laid up for many years. Take life easy; eat, drink and be merry."'"**

"The fool completely disregarded God," Steve said. "But at least he's planning ahead, as Joe pointed out. Many people never budget for the future."

"We cannot credit the rich fool with any wise decisions at all, Steve," Mrs. Coyne proclaimed hotly. "He's wasteful; he tore down perfectly good barns instead of renovating them. He was a hoarder. He was already rich, but he kept all of his wealth for himself when there must have been many needy people around him."

Steve's eyes widened, and he tried to speak twice before finally replying tightly, "Mrs. Coyne, the fool's key mistake wasn't saving excessively…it was his plan to fritter his savings away in one big, long party. With a work ethic like this, his money would quickly have disappeared."

Mrs. Coyne started to protest, but Bill interrupted. "Now, does anyone else have further comment up to this point?"

Samantha said, "I noticed that the man said he didn't have room. But he did have room in his first barns for what he *needed*. What he *wanted* was more room to keep all the extra God gave him. He got his *needs* mixed up with his *wants*. We do that too. We lie to ourselves, saying we *need* more for retirement, we need a bigger house, we need a better car. These are really just *wants*."

Jennifer rolled her eyes. "But it's foolish not to have a backup plan in case of financial catastrophe, Samantha. Having a reliable car saves a lot of time. Many people couldn't work at all without their vehicles. Parents couldn't drive their kids around."

Mrs. Coyne bristled. "Samantha is a single mom, Jennifer. She holds down a job and takes very good care of her son, all without a car."

"All right, folks," said Bill, "let's move on to verse 20. We've discussed many of the rich fool's sins. Among other things, he ignored God, lied to himself, and futilely planned to keep everything for himself.

Different members of the class described the rich fool's sin differently. Which seems closest to Jesus' meaning?

"The conclusion of this story features the only time God speaks directly in any of Christ's parables: **'But God said to him, "You fool! This very night your life will be demanded from you. Then who will get what you have prepared for yourself?"'** Bill surveyed the group.

Wayman grunted. "Hmph. God sure was in a hurry, wasn't He? 'This very night,' He says. That leaves no time to dawdle."

"He seems ferocious here," Cathy remarked. "The Lord wasn't fooling around."

"Indeed he was not," Bill agreed. "Nor is He today." Bill paused a moment before continuing. "Now, there's so much more we could discuss about this story, but overall, what is the point of the parable?"

I said, "I think Jesus made his point just before the parable. In verse 15, he warned, **'Watch out! Be on your guard against all kinds of greed; a man's life does not consist in the abundance of his possessions.'**"

"**All kinds of greed**?" Cathy looked puzzled. "You mean there's more than one kind?"

"Well, yeah," said Wayman. "In the next few verses, Jesus talked about worry, just like we saw in Matthew Greed isn't just wanting more; it's also worrying about not having a big enough safety net."

"What about wanting what someone else has?" I suggested. "The tenth commandment says, '**You shall not covet.**'"

Steve said, "Greed is attempting to get joy from material goods instead of from loving and serving God."

Sue quickly added, "Or putting your confidence in financial security, like the rich fool did."

"There are many powerful forms of greed," Bill summarized. "We should each take Jesus' warning personally to heart. If we don't think we're rich,

> Why is it true that "a man's life does not consist in the abundance of his possessions"? What does life consist of?

then we're not as likely to recognize subtle forms of greed in ourselves."

"How are we supposed to eliminate greed if it's so hard even to admit it?" Cathy's frown suddenly turned into a wide-eyed flash of insight. "Oh...I guess we're taking the first step right now—studying what the Bible has to say about it."

Steve nodded. "We can also ask ourselves the very questions the rich fool didn't ask: Am I honestly consulting God about financial decisions? Do I selfishly justify hoarding or unnecessary spending? Do I realize my money is really God's?"

"Accountability's pretty important, too." Wayman glanced at me. "I know there've been times these last few weeks when I would have let greed get its claws into me, except I knew some of you were praying for me." He continued quietly, "We can't beat it alone."

Samantha said, "And we can't beat it unless we keep on praying about it. I mean *keep on* praying. That's when God changes our hearts."

Bill said, "Those are all excellent suggestions. We must be constantly vigilant. I have a friend who is a prison guard—"

"Let me guess, Ron again?" I laughed.

"No, not this time," Bill said, returning my smile. "This friend works in the prison's video surveillance room, constantly monitoring television images from around the building. The guards have their routine checks of the inmates and the security systems. But that's exactly the problem—it becomes routine. When there's no action for awhile, they begin to just go through the motions. In the same way, we rich folks must deal urgently with any greed or love of money in our lives. Then we need to *stay* on guard. If not, we'll be ambushed."

Are there one or two "kinds of greed" which are especially deceptive for you? How can you be on guard against these?

Samantha said, "I think Joe's right—guarding against greed is Jesus' main point here. But look at verse 21 too. Jesus said the fool died, and then He finished the story with, '**This is how it will be with anyone who stores up things for himself but is not rich toward God**.' When I read that this week, I wondered what '**rich toward God**' meant, and it made me keep reading, and in the next part of the chapter Jesus talked about worry. That's what we get when we store up things for ourselves.

"Then in Luke 12:31, He said, '**But seek his kingdom, and these things will be given to you as well**'—just like we saw last week. I think we can be rich toward God by seeking His kingdom. We need to seek...well, we need to seek God Himself!"

"That sounds great," I said skeptically. "But I never did come up with an answer to Bill's question from last week—what does it mean, practically, to seek God's kingdom? What should I do today or tomorrow in order to become rich toward God?"

"Sell your possessions and give to the poor," Bill responded.

Jennifer sighed loudly, in annoyance. "That's your response to everything, Bill. It's impractical to just give and give."

"Those aren't my words," Bill answered evenly. "That's what Jesus said later in Luke 12, in verses 32-34:

> **[32]'Do not be afraid, little flock, for your Father has been pleased to give you the kingdom. [33]Sell your possessions and give to the poor. Provide purses for yourselves that will not wear out, a treasure in heaven that will not be exhausted, where no thief comes near and no moth destroys. [34]For where your treasure is, there your heart will be also.'**

"The fool should have given his crops to the poor. Then he would've had an inexhaustible heavenly treasure, a purse that would not wear out."

"I could use a purse with an eternal warranty." Samantha quipped. "I go through a new purse every year."

I thought of the tattered leather wallet in my pocket—the one Jennifer used to tell me to shoot and put out of its misery.

"Bill..." Steve was frowning and shaking his head. "I don't think unrestrained giving is the answer here. That's not responsible, godly stewardship. Under submission to God, a savings plan is beneficial in times of economic hardship. Even Jesus didn't condemn planning ahead. He said to focus

What new insights do you learn from this lesson about practically seeking God's kingdom (Matthew 6:33; Luke 12:31)?

on being rich toward God and not to store up for ourselves here on earth. But that doesn't mean we can't wisely save for the future!"

Steve turned to the middle of his Bible. "In fact, if we've finished exploring this passage, perhaps we could discuss the value of saving wisely?"

Bill nodded. Jennifer turned eagerly to a fresh notebook page.

The financial planner pressed on. "Is it necessarily self-ish to '**have plenty of things laid up for many years**,' as long as you don't put your security in them as the fool did?"

*Is it acceptable to "**have plenty of good things laid up for many years**" as long as you don't place your security in those things? Is it possible to do this?*

Bill shot back, "I doubt that it's possible to hoard wealth and *not* put your security in it."

"I disagree." Steve looked down at his Bible. "Proverbs 6:6-8 says, '**Go to the ant, you sluggard; consider its ways and be wise! It has no commander, no overseer or ruler, yet it stores its provisions in summer and gathers its food at harvest.**' Jesus didn't contradict Proverbs—His own inspired Word. Right after the parable of the rich fool, He warned against worry, not against saving."

The creases in Bill's forehead deepened. "But even the ant doesn't save years in advance—only for the time it knows it will be short on food. Proverbs 6 is more a warning against laziness than a blanket endorsement of saving."

Steve's voice began to rise in pitch. "But considering the ant's short life span, a single winter for him is comparable to our retirement years. I'm not talking about a life of idle, selfish pleasure; I'm talking about preparing in order not to be a burden on society or on our families. Having no retirement plan is risky."

Bill gesticulated with slightly shaking hands. "Yes, but it is human nature to rely on money for our security. Therefore, in the end, having no retirement plan is risky, but *having* one can be even riskier!"

"What about the story of Joseph in Egypt?" Steve challenged. "As Pharaoh's second-in-command, he put aside food during Egypt's seven years of plenty for use during the following seven years of famine. Joseph acted wisely with God's provisions."

How do you reconcile the parable of the rich fool with Proverbs 6:6-8?

Which is riskier for you—having savings or not having savings?

"Indeed he did," Bill replied immediately, "but contrast Joseph's story with the Israelites' forty-year journey in the desert. God gave his people manna to eat, but only one day's supply at a time—two days' when the Sabbath approached. God wanted the Israelites to rely on Him each and every day. If he'd given them food seven years in advance, they would soon have stopped relying on God."

"But the manna story is an unusual example of God's provision. God had a specific plan for the Israelites at that time."

"Joseph's was a special case too. How many of us see the future of our country in a dream?"

Steve heaved a great sigh, closed his Bible, and looked at the floor. He didn't see Bill wince and stop for breath.

Bill gathered himself quickly, then continued, emphasizing each word. "Saving is not wrong. But God's Word strongly and repeatedly warns that we're on dangerous ground when we focus on storing up money and possessions."

Steve appeared startled anew by Bill's fervency. "Bill, you're getting carried away with your emphasis on giving. We must responsibly steward God's money."

Bill bit back a retort, then leaned forward and lowered his head, both hands resting on his cane. Steve gave his head an exasperated little shake, crossed his arms, and stared out the window.

The rest of us shifted in our seats, uncertain how to break the awkward silence.

"Uh, guys?" I ventured. "So...how do we know how much savings is too much?"

For a few more seconds, Bill didn't move. Then he slowly raised his head, his eyes searching the room as if seeking orientation. After a moment, his pallid features lifted slightly, and he smiled a tired smile.

"Will you be surprised if I say you might be asking the wrong question? Instead of asking, 'How much should I save?' ask, 'How can I guard against greed?' In view of our God, who feeds the birds and clothes the lilies, we're in greater danger of greed than we are of deprivation."

With visible effort, Bill rallied to close the class. "Save some money, but beware of resting on your savings. Rest entirely on God's promised provision in the present and for the future. Extend your thoughts beyond your short time on earth and contemplate heaven. Being a Christian doesn't pay much, but the retirement plan is out of this world!"

Bill chuckled weakly at his own joke. The rest of us glanced at each other worriedly.

Bill continued, "Consult God about every financial decision, and evaluate your motives in His presence. Read and meditate on Bible passages like the ones we're studying in this class. Be continually and aggressively alert for greed in its many subtle disguises. Get an accountability partner who will challenge you in this area. Above all else, pray fervently against greed, as well as against all other evil from inside or from outside you. These matters are of the utmost urgency, as the rich fool discovered on the very night he laid his plans.

"Today, in Luke 12, we've seen a man pursuing an earthly estate. We've also seen the promise of an eternal inheritance, '**a treasure in heaven that will not be exhausted, where no thief comes near and no moth destroys**.' On which inheritance will you focus?"

Cathy nodded and smiled at Bill. Samantha and her grandmother were clasping each other's hands. Wayman cleared his throat nervously. Jennifer paused in her note-taking to glance admiringly at Steve.

"Now, if you'll excuse me..." Bill rose shakily from his chair and turned toward the door. Steve, suddenly concerned, sprang to his side to help. As they exited, I saw Bill pull a prescription bottle from his pocket.

A Brief Debrief

Even though that class session resulted in a near meltdown, it wasn't without impact. In fact, my own heart has been changed by the following two principles:

- Consult God about your financial decisions. We do this through prayer and by closely examining Scripture, among other godly decision-making practices.

- Check your motive for saving money. Is it out of anxiety or for selfish purposes? Or is it to love, serve, and glorify God in some way?

If, in God's wisdom, the rich fool had not died that very night, he still would never have experienced the peace and freedom he thought he had "bought." Anxiety and greed would have fuelled a perpetual restlessness. God cannot grasp our hands and lead us to freedom if we're clutching a whole bunch of earthly possessions in our hands. We need to let go of our money and goods and accept God's true life.

Cancel your plans to enlarge your barns. Instead, invest with God, and let Him use your wealth for eternal purposes.

Don't delay, for the situation is urgent. We never know when this life will end.

Deeper Study

What other Bible passages teach about saving? How do they add to your understanding of godly stewardship and the dangers of wealth? Here are a few to get you started: Proverbs 13:11, 21:20, 30:24-25.

The Hilarious Giver

As I ARRANGED THE CLASSROOM chairs in a circle, I prayed for the upcoming class. *God, unify this group with Your Spirit. Teach us Your thoughts about money and joyful generosity.*

I also thought back on my meeting earlier that week with Wayman. With his encouragement, I had finally taken the plunge and committed to giving one tenth of my gross income off the top before expending any other money from each paycheque. I had dropped the first such cheque in the offering plate not one hour earlier, and my wallet seemed substantially lighter.

Then I realized that my heart felt lighter too. *I guess generosity really can be joyful.* Then I frowned. *But will it last?*

Mrs. Coyne and Samantha were next to arrive. Samantha smiled warmly at me before dropping her eyes. I thought I saw Mrs. Coyne hiding a grin.

Right on their heels came Wayman, then Jennifer, notebook and Bible in hand, dressed and primped for success.

When Cathy entered, she seemed more troubled than I could ever remember seeing her. I wondered if her pregnancy and family demands were draining her.

Finally, a few minutes late, Bill and Steve arrived together, Bill hobbling, Steve holding his arm.

"Sorry, gang," Bill apologized. "When I woke up this morning, parts of my body hurt that I didn't even know I had." He settled slowly and gingerly into his chair.

We opened with a few minutes of prayer, then Bill announced, "The first order of business today is some housecleaning. I owe all of you, and especially my brother Steve, my deepest apologies. Last Sunday, I behaved very poorly in my disagreement with Steve over savings and giving. God doesn't expect all of His children to see eye to eye, but He does call us to deal with our disagreements in an agreeable, patient, loving manner. I hurt Steve, and I may have hurt some of you when I lost my temper. I'm sorry and I hope you will all forgive me."

Before anyone could respond, Steve jumped in. "Actually, I think I was the greater offender. I came to that realization after a long talk with Bill last Sunday evening. As we talked, I came to see more of this good man's heart, and after prayerfully looking at quite a number of Scripture passages together, I can now see that, in the name of stewardship and wise financial planning, perhaps I've been limiting my faith and joy in God. Our Lord gives exuberantly, in ways that don't balance on a balance sheet, and He calls us to give the same way."

Dismay spread across Jennifer's face.

Steve continued, "I still advocate strongly for wise planning and saving—" beside him, Bill nodded vigorously, "but not at the expense of generous, extravagant, faith-filled giving. I hope you'll all forgive me, too, for the way I mishandled the conversation last week."

All of us murmured words of encouragement—all except Jennifer, who sulked in silence.

"Thank you, everyone," said Bill. "Now, let's get on with this week's study. The passage is a little long, but let's still read it twice. Wayman, would you read first for us? It's 2 Corinthians 8:1-12 and 9:6-8."

Wayman nodded and read aloud:

> [1]And now, brothers, we want you to know about the grace that God has given the Macedonian churches. [2]Out of the most severe trial, their overflowing joy and their extreme poverty welled up in rich generosity. [3]For I testify that they gave as much as they were able, and even beyond their ability. Entirely on their own, [4]they urgently pleaded with us for the privilege of sharing in this service to the saints. [5]And they did not do as we expected, but they gave themselves first to the Lord and then to us in keeping with God's will. [6]So we urged Titus, since he had earlier made a beginning, to bring also to completion this act of grace on your part. [7]But just as you excel in everything—in faith, in speech, in knowledge, in complete earnestness and in your love for us—see that you also excel in this grace of giving.
>
> [8]I am not commanding you, but I want to test the sincerity of your love by comparing it with the earnestness of others. [9]For you know the grace of our Lord Jesus Christ, that though he was rich, yet for your sakes he became poor, so that you through his poverty might become rich.
>
> [10]And here is my advice about what is best for you in this matter. Last year you

> were the first not only to give but also to
> have the desire to do so. [11]Now finish the
> work, so that your eager willingness to do
> it may be matched by your completion of
> it, according to your means. [12]For if the
> willingness is there, the gift is acceptable
> according to what one has, not according
> to what he does not have.

"And now the verses in chapter 9," Wayman said.

> [6]Remember this: Whoever sows sparingly
> will also reap sparingly, and whoever
> sows generously will also reap generously.
> [7]Each man should give what he has de-
> cided in his heart to give, not reluctantly
> or under compulsion, for God loves a
> cheerful giver. [8]And God is able to make
> all grace abound to you, so that in all
> things at all times, having all that you
> need, you will abound in every good
> work.

After Wayman finished reading, Bill began, "I call this
week's study 'The Hilarious Giver.' In 9:7, Paul writes,
'**God loves a cheerful giver.**' The Greek word for 'cheerful' is *hilaros*, which I believe is the root of our English
word *hilarious*.

"Now, a little historical background, folks: The apostle
Paul founded a church in the city of Corinth, in modern-day
Greece. He kept in touch with the believers by writing several letters to them, including 1 and 2 Corinthians. The Corinthians were quite wealthy. On the other hand, the Christian church in Jerusalem was desperately poor at the time,
probably due to persecution and local famine. So, to assist
those in Jerusalem, to honour Christ, and to generate unity
for all the Christian churches, Paul organized a special

monetary collection to benefit the Jerusalem church. The Corinthians agreed to participate in the collection, but their resolve wavered. So, in 2 Corinthians 8 and 9, Paul addressed their reluctance."

Several heads nodded, so he continued, "Joe, would you read the passages again for us now?"

When I had finished reading, Bill scanned his notes, then said, "Macedonia was a Greek province near Corinth, and the churches there were poor in contrast with the wealthy Corinthians. Yet in 8:2, we see that the Macedonians contributed to the collection for Jerusalem with '**rich generosity**.' So, my first question today is, What was the source of the Macedonians' rich generosity?"

Cathy seemed to stir from a deep reverie and answered slowly, "It's right there in verse 2, Bill. The Macedonians were experiencing a severe trial, out of which their overwhelming joy and extreme poverty produced this generosity." She frowned for a moment. "I'm always mystified as to how some people can be joyful when they are persecuted, severely handicapped, or extremely poor."

"Extreme poverty *is* a most severe trial," Mrs. Coyne lamented. "When you don't have enough money for basic needs, discouragement and selfishness are right around the corner."

"That's true for some folks," Wayman agreed. "But for some, I think it's actually easier to give out of poverty. Poor people just aren't as overwhelmed with materialism and greed. It's easier for them to feel free to give."

Steve shook his head and said, "That's not true. Impoverished individuals are just as materialistic as rich people. The poor are envious of what they *don't* have."

"Hmph. Maybe." Wayman shrugged. "But I think it's easier for poor people to share, because they identify more with people in need."

Cathy's frown deepened as she stared at her Bible.

Scenes from my mission trip to South America came to mind, and I said, "I've noticed that the less people have, the less they want. Some poor people are generous despite their poverty. Others, like the Macedonians, are generous partly *because* of their poverty. In fact, a recent study I read found that, generally, the richer people are, the lower the percentage of income they give to charity."

Steve responded, "Well, that's just because when someone in extreme poverty gives a small amount, it's actually a large percentage of their income."

"That's true, Steve," I said. "That's true."

In their hilarious generosity, what did the Macedonians lose? What did they gain?

Do you identify more closely with the Corinthians or the Macedonians? Why?

To no one in particular, Cathy said, "Did you notice that the Macedonians didn't have to be told to give?" She chewed the end of her pen. "*They* were the ones who *asked* to give. They **'urgently pleaded'** with Paul and his associates **'for the privilege of sharing in this service to the saints.'** For them, giving to people in need was a privilege."

Wayman nodded. "Pretty radical, huh?"

After a moment's thoughtful silence, Samantha said, "Bill, you asked where the Macedonians' generosity came from. Verse 1 says, **'We want you to know about the grace that God has given the Macedonian churches.'** Grandma says that God's grace is His unconditional giving."

The Macedonians considered giving a privilege. Do you consider giving a privilege?

"That's right," said Bill. "The Greek word for 'grace' is related to the word for 'gift.' It's *charis,* from which we derive our English *charity.*"

Samantha smiled. "Then that makes sense. They were so poor that they were especially grateful for God's grace. They were generous with money because He had been so generous in other, bigger ways."

Bill shifted to face Samantha and gestured with both hands. "Isn't it amazing? God's grace to the Macedonians meant that their severe trial ultimately produced rich generosity!"

Samantha wasn't finished. "Yeah. In fact, grace is all over these two chapters. I underlined it wherever I found it. In 8:6-7, Paul talked about giving itself as grace, and told us to '**excel in this grace of giving.**' In verse 9, Paul says that Jesus showed grace when He gave His life for us." She paused and said quietly, "That's just great," then continued, "And later, in 9:8, God's grace gives us everything we need and helps us '**abound in every good work.**' Then in verse 14, which we didn't read aloud, it says that our giving is itself God's grace to us—something He gives us the ability to do." She looked up, glowing, and pushed her glasses back on her nose.

"That's not all," said Bill. "Paul wrapped up in 9:15, saying, '**Thanks be to God for his indescribable gift!**' You're right, Samantha. God's own generous grace is the bottom-line reason the Macedonians gave so freely and eagerly. These verses get me all excited too."

"Well, some of them get me all offended!" Mrs. Coyne's angry tone caught us by surprise. "I don't like the way Paul

How have you experienced God's incredible grace?

manipulated the Corinthians into giving. Look at 8:8: '**I am not commanding you, but I want to test the sincerity of your love by comparing it with the earnestness of others.**' How do you think they felt after he judged their love by comparing their giving to someone else's?" Her pitch rose to a screech. "Imagine our denomination president sending us a letter that said, 'Dear Church X, I'll believe you really love Jesus when you give as much to missions as Church Y.' Is this a competition?"

Bill responded quickly, "No, Sue, it's not. Paul simply held the Macedonians up as an example for the Corinthians.

Positive modeling is one of the ways we '**spur one another on toward love and good deeds**,' as we read in Hebrews 10:24. And Paul wasn't comparing the dollar amount, but rather, the earnestness of their hearts."

Mrs. Coyne's glare softened slightly. Bill went on, "In fact, let me ask all of you: What do we learn about the actual amount the Macedonians gave?"

I quickly checked for any numbers or similar clues. Finding none, I replied, "In 8:3 it says, '**They gave as much as they were able, and even beyond their ability**.'" I thought for a moment. "'**Even beyond their ability**'? That sounds extreme."

Steve grinned sheepishly. "If we had studied this last week, I would have said flatly that giving beyond your ability is unwise and unbiblical. But Paul praises the Macedonians for doing just that. However, I still think that we have to be careful. Giving what we can't afford would cause debt, and Proverbs warns strongly against debt."

"But how many of us are in debt because of giving?" Samantha asked. "Most debts are from spending on ourselves, not from giving too much. What you said sounds like…well, I'm sorry, but it just sounds like an excuse not to give in a way that takes real faith."

Samantha shrank back slightly, anticipating Steve's rejoinder. But when Steve simply raised his eyebrows and nodded, she relaxed.

Amazing! I thought. *This shy, uneducated girl just taught a professional financial planner something about money.* I suddenly realized that since the first day of class, I had not released Samantha from my initial perceptions of a not-so-bright wallflower. I looked at her with new appreciation.

Jennifer had been silent since class began, but now she shifted in her seat and said, "Well, even though the Macedonians gave more than they could afford, I notice that Paul didn't tell the Corinthians to do this. In verses 11 and 12, he told them to give '**according to your means**,' not according to what they didn't have." She appealed to the group, focusing especially on Steve, but studiously avoiding Samantha.

Bill responded, "As I've said before, Jennifer, the Bible doesn't have a giving formula. The teachings and examples we see throughout the Old and New Testaments seem to vary widely, all the way from giving 'reasonably' to giving everything. If we approach this study by looking for *the one* answer, we run the danger of becoming legalistic. In any case, I suspect that all of these giving standards are beyond what most of us are doing now.

"The one common thread is that all hilarious givers, like the Macedonians, considered giving to be a privilege. They did not strive to give a minimum; they wanted to give the maximum, and even beyond. God's grace produced that desire in them. Full of grace, joyful even in poverty, they gave *themselves* first to the Lord. Then they were eager also to give what they possessed."

FYI: For teaching on regular giving in proportion to one's means, see 1 Corinthians 16:1-2. First Corinthians is Paul's earlier letter to these same people.

Jennifer started to speak, but then thought better of it and stared sullenly at the floor.

"Bill…" Steve raised his index finger. "Could I add that accountability is the key that helps many people break through to faith-filled giving?"

I glanced at Wayman, then said, "Steve's right. I'm learning, too, how important accountability is. We all need someone to spur us on—a small group, a spouse, a friend…anyone who will be honest and trustworthy."

I looked again at Wayman. He gave me a quick, straight-faced wink.

Mrs. Coyne muttered, "Accountability may be good, but to me, Paul sounds like a loan shark sending out his 'brothers' to forcibly collect what's owed."

What does giving "according to your means" look like in practical terms?

What does it mean to give yourself first to the Lord, then to others?

We all laughed, and Mrs. Coyne managed a grim smile.

She shook her head in exasperation. "Maybe I'm overstating the situation a little, but all through these two chapters, Paul seems so shaming, so..." She closed her wrinkled eyelids tightly, then opened them. "So...*parental.* Who is he—their father?"

"I know what you mean, Sue," I said. "Most of the accountability relationships in my past have been bad experiences because we became heavy-handed without the balancing grace toward each other. Now I'm learning that, while healthy accountability isn't always comfortable—sometimes it's downright grim—still, you always know that the other person accepts and loves you, as God does. I think that's the relationship Paul had toward the Corinthians." A new thought occurred to me. "Maybe he *was* a little like a dad—a spiritual father that the Corinthians knew would never stop loving them, even when he disciplined them."

Did Paul contradict himself by "strong-arming" the Corinthians into giving, then teaching that '**God loves a cheerful giver**' (9:7)?

Jennifer couldn't give up without attempting one more shot. "Bill, I'm still bothered by the fact that we're not discussing more specific guidelines for giving from the Bible."

Bill sighed, then extended his hands toward Jennifer in warm appeal. "Jennifer, in God's great wisdom, the Bible simply doesn't emphasize specific guidelines in this area—not for New Covenant givers. The most important specific aspect of giving taught in 2 Corinthians is *actually doing it.* The Corinthians had dragged their feet. So Paul prodded them, '**Now finish the work**.'

"Their gift only became reality when they finally completed it. That's when good intentions graduated into action. It's *not* only the thought that counts. *Do it.* And do it until you are free from mastery by materialism. Do it until you experience the joy of God's grace flowing through you to others.

"Too many specifics would distract us from the more important heart attitude. Specifics are easy. The hard, but crucial, part is letting God fill our hearts with love and grace toward Him and others, so that giving of our money, of our time...of *ourselves*...becomes second nature. It's not our money or time, anyways. Don't give up. Pray for God's grace to fill you, and giving will become a privilege, just as it was for the Macedonians."

Bill glanced down at his notes. "Which bring up our last question for today. In 9:7, Paul wrote, '**Each man should give what he has decided in his heart to give, not reluctantly or under compulsion, for God loves a cheerful giver.**' How do we give cheerfully and joyfully if we are reluctant or feel obligated?"

Mrs. Coyne's cheeks puffed up twice as she tried to put her thoughts into words. "Well, Paul's saying clearly that we shouldn't give unless we feel good about it—until our heart leads us to give."

Bill smiled and turned toward Mrs. Coyne. "Yes, Sue, at first glance this verse seems to teach that. Unfortunately, that interpretation is based on a common misunderstanding of the word *heart*. In both the Old and New Testaments, the heart represents the entire inner person—intellect, will, and emotions. We often confuse this with the way our culture uses the word *heart*—namely, to represent solely our emotions, our feelings. When Paul wrote '**decided in his heart**,' he was referring to an action of the will, whether the feelings went along with it or not. He wasn't telling us to wait for our emotions to say yes."

How do your feelings affect your decisions to give?

How do your decisions to give affect your feelings?

At this, a silent tear ran down Cathy's cheek and made a barely audible *pat* as it dropped onto the page of her Bible. Bill's brow creased, and he turned toward Cathy.

We all waited several seconds. Then Cathy looked up, eyes brimming, not focusing on anyone in particular. "I think…" She looked back down, then took a deep breath. To her Bible she said, "I think I know now why giving has never been something I really enjoyed. As important as my family is, I think I've been putting them ahead of God. I've always calculated what we would need each month, and added a little extra to the total as a safety margin. Then what was left was fair game for God. And I always gave with fear—fear that I might have figured wrong and we might not have enough after all."

More tears ran down her face. She wiped absently at them. "I need to have a talk with Bob. I see now that we're missing out. I want us to be hilarious givers, and I want us to trust God to take care of our family's needs in ways that we can't understand ahead of time."

Bill nodded slowly, but didn't speak. Cathy continued, "I was checking my heart each time to see what amount didn't feel too scary to give. But that's not joy. I want us to *decide in our hearts* to give more and then trust that God's joy will come." A small smile appeared. "In fact, it's already here." She closed her eyes and wept quietly.

Samantha reached over and put an arm around Cathy's shoulders.

After a moment, Bill said quietly, "I'm happy for you, Cathy. You've just made one of your life's most significant breakthroughs. You've overcome fear and come into joy. It wasn't easy. It didn't happen by itself. You chose to obey God. His Spirit changed your heart. And that's how you won the battle."

Cathy looked up at Bill and nodded.

Bill scanned the circle. "Each of us has a different reason for our reluctance to give. For Cathy it has been fear. For others it might be greed or love of money. But victory boils down to a decision, not to a feeling. That decision becomes much easier when we gaze upon the grace, the rich generosity of God."

He paused, then said in a subdued voice, "I think we should finish on that note. Our homework for the week is to read all of 2 Corinthians 9 and ask ourselves: What results did Paul promise if the Corinthians would give cheerfully and generously?

"Also, spend time reading next week's passage, preparing to discuss what is sometimes called the 'Health and Wealth Gospel' or 'Prosperity Theology.'"

Prosperity. Health and Wealth. I pondered these as I got up and moved toward the door. Those are some of the most controversial words in Christendom!

As I distractedly walked by Samantha and her grandmother, Samantha caught my eye with a smile. She leaned close and whispered, "See you next week."

Uncertain what to say, I returned the smile, nodded, and made my way out of the room.

A Brief Debrief

Second Corinthians 8-9 is rich with principles pertaining to our handling of money. To me, these are the three most memorable principles from these chapters:

- God's grace is the root source of our generosity.

- Giving is only fruitful if the gift is completed.

- God loves a hilarious giver—one who finds joy as the fruit of determined obedience.

Today in our culture, the vast majority of us are more like the wealthy Corinthians than the poverty-stricken Macedonians. We have unprecedented ability and opportunity to contribute to the poor and to various outreach efforts. What might God do through us if we were to combine our great wealth with the selfless, giving hearts of the Macedonians? How might He use our lives if we were to give ourselves to Him...if we were to be overwhelmed with His joy and grace?

How confident are you that "God is able to make all grace abound to you, so that in all things at all times, having all that you need, you will abound in every good work"? How can you become more confident in God's ability to provide for you this generously?

Is it possible to give too much? Is it possible to focus too much on giving?

Deeper Study

Study the portions of 2 Corinthians 8-9 that weren't discussed in this lesson. What additional principles do you find regarding biblical giving? In particular, read 9:6-15 and find as many results as you can that Paul promises will come about when the Corinthians have given generously.

Plans to Prosper You?

THE AROMA OF FRESHLY BAKED BREAD filled the classroom. Bill had finally made good on his promise. I was grateful that I had missed breakfast that morning. It left me with even more room to sample the four kinds of bread and the huge variety of jellies, preserves, and other spreads provided by Cathy and Mrs. Coyne.

In the midst of the happy hubbub, Jennifer sat in her own dome of silence, nibbling half-heartedly at a small slice of whole wheat with garlic butter.

Bill seemed more sickly than ever. He smiled weakly and declined every time someone offered him a sampling of his own baked goods.

Samantha had brought a visitor, a man who looked to be about my age.

"Everyone, this is Max." Sam gestured toward her guest. "He's an assistant manager at Burger Queen, and when I told him about our discussions, he asked if he could come."

"Yeah," said Max. "And thanks for having me." His enthusiasm and intensity struck me immediately. "In fact, when Sam told me you studied 2 Corinthians 8-9 last week, I couldn't wait to come. Those two chapters have some of my favourite verses in the Bible. Like 9:6, which says that if we sow generously, we will reap a prosperous harvest. And then in verse 10, if we plant a seed, God will give us a harvest of righteousness—an abundance of good things— money, health, happiness…all to God's glory! God wants us to prosper, and Christians desperately need freedom from the bonds of poverty and debt."

Max paused, beaming, as though waiting for a chorus of amens.

The silence, however, was broken only by a few scattered coughs and the sounds of people shifting in their seats. Jennifer slowly opened her notebook, a look of fresh interest on her face.

After an uncomfortable interval, Wayman spoke up. "Uh, well, Max, I'm glad you came, and I'm sure you know more about some of these Bible verses than I do…" He looked at his own open Bible. "But don't you think the **'harvest of your righteousness'** in verse 10 means a lot more than money? I mean, Jesus died for us so we would change the way we live. So we would *be* righteous and *act* righteously. I think that's the harvest Paul meant. I don't think he was talking about a pile of cash and nice things."

Max looked surprised. "But verse 11 says, **'You will be made rich in every way so that you can be generous on every occasion.'** God makes us wealthy so we can give more."

"You know, Max," Samantha said softly, "I was thinking that same thing when Grandma and I sat down to do our homework this week. Oh, I think I forgot to tell you, Bill asked us to study chapter 9 a little more." She unfolded a sheet of notebook paper and laid it flat on her Bible. "But when we looked at the results Paul promised would come if the Corinthians gave generously, we saw results like good works, thanksgiving, meeting of needs, and praise to God." She frowned at her paper for a moment. "Yeah, I guess some of the things Paul promised could be taken to mean financial blessing, but I really don't think that's the main thing he had in mind."

A slight furrow creased Max's brow, but he remained silent.

What does it mean to be "rich in every way"?

"Thank you for being so willing to share, Max," said Bill. "I can see that you love the Lord, and we're very glad you're with us. We've had our share of differing viewpoints in this class, and it would appear we've come across yet another. But I would remind everyone—" he took in every face, "that our attitude toward each other is to be loving and accepting, even when we disagree."

Without warning, Bill curled up in a spasm of coughing. He pulled out a handkerchief while Steve supported him with an arm around his shoulders. Cathy rushed out of the room and brought back a cup of water, which Bill sipped gratefully.

After a minute, Steve asked, "Would you like me to open in prayer?"

Bill nodded, and coughed only a few more times while we prayed.

When we all looked up, Bill took a deep breath, smiled, and said, "I apologize, folks. I've been a little under the weather this week. But I'm better now." He looked down at his notes. "So let's all turn to today's main passages in 1 Timothy 6, verses 3-12 and 17-19. Max, would you do us the favour of reading these verses, twice if you don't mind?"

Max found the passage and read aloud:

³If anyone teaches false doctrines and does not agree to the sound instruction of

our Lord Jesus Christ and to godly teaching, [4]he is conceited and understands nothing. He has an unhealthy interest in controversies and quarrels about words that result in envy, strife, malicious talk, evil suspicions [5]and constant friction between men of corrupt mind, who have been robbed of the truth and who think that godliness is a means to financial gain.

[6]But godliness with contentment is great gain. [7]For we brought nothing into the world, and we can take nothing out of it. [8]But if we have food and clothing, we will be content with that. [9]People who want to get rich fall into temptation and a trap and into many foolish and harmful desires that plunge men into ruin and destruction. [10]For the love of money is a root of all kinds of evil. Some people, eager for money, have wandered from the faith and pierced themselves with many griefs.

[11]But you, man of God, flee from all this, and pursue righteousness, godliness, faith, love, endurance and gentleness. [12]Fight the good fight of the faith. Take hold of the eternal life to which you were called when you made your good confession in the presence of many witnesses....

[17]Command those who are rich in this present world not to be arrogant nor to put their hope in wealth, which is so uncertain, but to put their hope in God, who richly provides us with everything for our enjoyment. [18]Command them to do good, to be rich in good deeds, and to be generous and willing to share. [19]In this way

**they will lay up treasure for themselves as
a firm foundation for the coming age, so
that they may take hold of the life that is
truly life.**

After Max read the passage again, Bill said, "Paul wrote
this letter to Timothy, a young pastor at Ephesus under
Paul's tutelage. Even though we're reading someone else's
mail, we know it is also God's message to us, because it
contains teachings that Paul meant to be conveyed to the
whole church. Parts of chapter 6, directed to '**those who
are rich**,' are especially for us, because, as we've already
agreed, we are wealthy too.

"So, let's begin with this query: What did Paul warn
against in verses 3-5?"

"The Health and Wealth
Gospel and its false prosperity
teachers!" Mrs. Coyne proclaimed shrilly, her stern gaze
fixed on Max. "They preach
mostly to get money for themselves. Our God doesn't pay us
money for being good. 'Name it
and claim it' is more like 'blab it
and grab it'—"

*We've come back often to
the truth that we are
among the wealthiest peo-
ple in history. This is so
hard for us to believe that it
bears repeating. Take a
moment and ask God to
prepare you to hear God's
teaching through the ears
of a rich person.*

Bill broke in firmly, "Thank you, Sue, but please remember what I said about showing a loving attitude toward
others." His tone softened, "It sounds as though you've had
some painful past experiences relating to these issues. I respect that and I'm sorry for it, but we must be careful to let
the Bible speak for itself, rather than reading our experience into God's Word."

Bill leaned heavily on his cane as he shifted in his chair.
"Now, on the other hand, Paul does open by confronting
those who teach false doctrine—that is, in Paul's words,

anything that doesn't agree with '**the sound instruction of our Lord Jesus Christ and to godly teaching**.'"

He coughed twice into his handkerchief and blinked for a moment. "Now, I normally try to let the class do most of the talking, but as a spiritual leader—as a shepherd, you might say—I feel obligated to underscore Paul's warning. Today we have many misguided preachers who claim to be teaching God's Word, but whose sermons are typically based on half verses, poor translations, or misinterpretations that take the Bible's truths out of context. These false doctrines directly contradict Scripture. What makes me most angry is that their teachings confuse and mislead many earnest believers—" his eyes flicked unconsciously in Max's direction, "who swallow false teachings because of a kernel of truth buried in each one."

"Or because of the personal charisma of the speaker," Cathy added.

Wayman scratched his beard. "You know, I've spent my share of time going after financial gain in lots of ungodly ways, but I can't say I've ever thought that '**godliness is a means to financial gain**,' like some of those false teachers did in verse 5."

Our leader cleared his throat and said, "Good insight, Wayman. Apparently, Paul knew of some teachers who tried to merge their so-called 'godliness' with the pursuit of wealth. Let's look ahead to verses 6-8. What does true godliness result in?"

How do we determine if a teaching is right?

Is godliness ever a means to financial gain? Explain.

Samantha answered, "When we put godliness together with contentment, it's '**great gain**.'" She pushed back her glasses. To my surprise, I discovered that I found the mannerism endearing.

"And he started verse 6 with the word *but*," Mrs. Coyne added, her finger raised. "So godly gain is different from financial gain."

Cathy said, "Verses 7-8 say that godliness is remembering that we can't take earthly goods to heaven. We are to be content with food and clothing." A smile spread slowly over her face. "I'm just now figuring out what that means. I should tell you all that Bob and I talked this week. He still wants to be cautious and make sure that our needs are met, but he agreed to increase our giving. So we'll see how content and trusting we can learn to be."

Max shook his head and burst out, "But Paul didn't say being wealthy is bad. In fact, Proverbs 10:22 says, '**The blessing of the LORD brings wealth, and he adds no trouble to it.**' God wants the best for us, and isn't being wealthy better?"

"That's a good question, Max," I replied. "But the guy who wrote Proverbs 30:8-9 saw potential danger at both extremes. He said, **Give me neither poverty nor riches, but give me only my daily bread. Otherwise, I may have too much and disown you and say, 'Who is the Lord?' Or I may become poor and steal, and so dishonor the name of my God.**"

When I looked up and saw Samantha watching me, she blushed and dropped her gaze.

Max sounded discouraged as he said, "But I've always been taught that God wants us to be wealthy. In Psalm 35:27, David wrote, '**The LORD be exalted, who delights in the prosperity of his servant.**' Then there's Jeremiah 29:11. It says, '"**For I know the plans I have for you," declares the LORD, "plans to prosper you and not to harm you, plans to give you hope and a future."**'"

> **FYI**: Frequently the Old Testament does show God basing material rewards on people's behaviour. The New Testament emphasizes this type of reward much less. Our God does not change, but He has total freedom to deal with different people or groups differently, as He sees fit.

"Jesus had plenty of chances to tell people they should be rich," said Wayman. "But He didn't. In fact, He said it was near impossible for a rich man to get into heaven."

"But I thought Jesus was rich." Max looked puzzled. "Several wealthy women gave Him so much money that He needed Judas to be His treasurer. And in John 1, doesn't it say that Jesus owned his own house?"

A small gasp came from Bill's direction. He slowly ran a hand over his tired face. "I'm sorry, Max, but I think you've been misled. In John 1, the house to which Jesus invited the men was only the place He was staying at the time—not a house He owned. This is exactly the misuse of Scripture that Paul warned against." Bill waited a moment, but Max didn't respond. "That brings us back to our main passage. Next question: What happens to people who want to get rich?"

In response, Samantha simply read verse 9 aloud: **"People who want to get rich fall into temptation and a trap and into many foolish and harmful desires that plunge men into ruin and destruction."**

Here Max spoke up. "But a lot of people want money so they can support Christian ministries or give gifts when God tells them to. Of course, I can see that greediness for yourself is bad, but I think the most important question is *Why* do you want to be rich?"

Cathy said, "I'm sure motive is important, but this warning doesn't distinguish between selfish people and people who want to serve God. '**Temptation and a trap…foolish and harmful desires…ruin and destruction**'—these are the dangers for *any* '**people who want to get rich**.'"

Max shook his head in confusion. "My pastor would call that a poverty mentality. He says that people who reject God's gift of prosperity will go into bondage to poverty and debt."

"Debt doesn't come from a poverty mentality," Bill said gently. "It usually comes from overspending or unwise investments. In our wealthy society, no one knows the meaning of *true* poverty. Prosperity theologians push us to look for wealth, but we already have it.

"I've shared with the class a few stories about a friend of mine named Ron. For many years he lived only to get rich. He claimed that his motive was a righteous one. But his quest for money—whatever the motive—kept him from experiencing gratitude for the abundance God had already given him." Pain flickered across Bill's face. "Indeed, as Paul says here in verse 10, Ron pierced himself with many griefs—depression, damaged relationships, deep wounds in those nearest him…" he trailed off, staring out the window.

Quietly, Steve said, "In that same verse, Paul wrote, **'The love of money is a root of all kinds of evil.'** As a financial planner, I've counselled thousands of clients, and I've seen love of money as a cause, or at least a partial cause, of a wide variety of problems—marital failure, family discord, business disputes, departure from the faith…and on a global scale, wars, disease, starvation…"

"For the last ten or twenty years, I was having a love affair with money." Wayman spoke to the floor. "When God got hold

What kinds of evil can grow out of the love of money?

of me just a little while ago, I wondered if I should quit selling cars. I can always feel money tugging at my heart. It's still a battle."

Bill began to perk up. "And I'm glad you're still in that business, Wayman. You're shining God's light in dark places." Another coughing fit struck, but after a moment, Bill controlled it and continued, "Next question, then: If we're not to pursue riches, what should we pursue?"

Mrs. Coyne began to read, "**Pursue righteousness, godliness, faith, love, endurance and gentleness…** Not money."

"We don't have to pursue money!" Max exclaimed. "It will come to us if we obey God with our seed. We must give generously. Ecclesiastes 11:1 says, '**Cast your bread upon the waters, for after many days you will find it again.'** God always has more that He wants to give us!"

137

Steve frowned. "But Ecclesiastes also says there's a downside to wanting more." He searched for a moment. "Here it is. Ecclesiastes 5:10-12:

> **[10]Whoever loves money never has money enough; whoever loves wealth is never satisfied with his income. This too is meaningless. [11]As goods increase, so do those who consume them. And what benefit are they to the owner except to feast his eyes on them? [12]The sleep of a laborer is sweet, whether he eats little or much, but the abundance of a rich man permits him no sleep.**

"Financial prosperity may be a gift from God, but God's other blessings are far better—blessings like His grace, peace, righteousness, faith, love…"

List some ways God has blessed you. Which are the best types of blessings?

How content would you be with only food and clothing?

Max didn't respond, but continued to examine his Bible carefully.

Mrs. Coyne said, "Don't forget about those last three verses—1 Timothy 6:17-19. The rich should not be arrogant nor hope in wealth. I think most wealthy people do depend on their riches instead of on God. It's better by far to be poor, because—"

"You guys don't get it! Do you?"

We all turned toward Jennifer. Her exasperated outburst had caught us off guard. "It's right there in front of you. Open your eyes!" She thumped her Bible. "Verse 17 says God '**richly provides us with everything for our enjoyment.**' God wants us to enjoy good things. '**Everything,**' Paul says."

She paused while the rest of us checked the wording. "Paul didn't say, 'Command those who are rich to be

138

ashamed of their wealth and give away every last penny.' That's what some of you—" here she looked pointedly at Bill, then me, "would like us all to think. I don't go in for all of this prosperity stuff, but sometimes I think it's a lot closer to reality than this group's collective thinking."

Stunned silence reigned, broken only when Bill sneezed loudly, then cleared his throat. He seemed at a loss for words, but finally he said, sadly, "I'm sorry you feel that way, Jennifer. I'd take time to respond to your concerns, but, for one, we have already dealt with each of them extensively in earlier classes, and I'd simply be repeating myself. And, for another, I'm afraid we're out of time." He scanned the circle of dazed faces, his own eyes glazed with fatigue. "Thank you, everyone, for participating in the discussion. Thank you for coming, Max. I hope to see everyone next week."

Is Bill just going to give up that easily? I thought in dismay. This conversation isn't finished.

Most of the class members stood quietly and prepared to leave. Max looked troubled, and I overheard him say something to Bill about "a few things to think over."

While the others filed out, Jennifer moved slowly through a world of her own, all of her energy spent in that one burst. Bill also took his time putting away his notes and mustering his strength.

In that moment I made an impulsive decision. I took three determined steps across the circle and faced Jennifer, who was halfway out of her chair. "Jenn, you're getting yourself into some serious trouble with God." She dropped back into her chair, not looking me in the eye. "You're as arrogant as those rich people Paul was confronting. I've started to give sacrificially, and so has Wayman...and Cathy. Now I know Bill has been right all along, and, frankly, you're wrong!"

My words echoed around the room. Jenn placed her elbows on her knees and rested her face in her hands.

139

"Well?" I half shouted. "Aren't you going to—"

"Joe." Bill's feeble voice stopped me. He coughed for a few seconds, regained his breath, and said, "I've felt the same way you do right now, many times in my life. I can't count the times I've spotted an irritating speck in the eye of a brother or sister in Christ, and I thought it was my duty to point it out." He shrugged. "Sometimes it was. But I could show you a whole stack of personalized planks that I later realized had been protruding from my own eye, even as I had been trying to 'help' my friends."

Jennifer didn't move.

Bill continued, "You've spoken very harshly to Jennifer. And it's obvious that she's feeling very discouraged right now."

Jennifer looked up at Bill. Her eyes were moist.

My stomach sank. Suddenly the zeal left me, replaced by a truckload of shame and embarrassment. "Um…yeah," was all I could think to say.

Bill's gaze shifted from me to Jennifer, and I saw a tear make its way through the maze of cracks and wrinkles that surrounded his eyes. For a moment he only sat watching her. She dropped her eyes.

"My dear Jennifer," Bill said finally, "you've done so many good things for God. But you know…don't you?" He paused. "One thing remains. One very important thing."

Jennifer stared at the floor for many more heartbeats. Then, without looking up, she said in a tired voice, "What I should have known is that it would eventually come down to this." She glanced up at me, then looked steadily at Bill. Her features hardened. "Bill, if your idea of spirituality means I have to abide by some vague notion of 'joyful generosity,' rather than clear-cut instructions for giving, then I don't want any part of it. If you mean I can't have nice things in my life and that I can't enjoy God's material blessings, then I'm sorry, but your Christ is not the same as mine."

"But, Jennifer." Bill held out a quavering hand. "Rules and regulations are cruel taskmasters. Only God is the gracious Master who gives you '**the life that is truly life.**'*"

"I have my life!" She rose suddenly from her chair. "God *is* in it, and He's not the demanding God of deprivation you make Him out to be." She turned her back and walked away.

"But that's not—" Bill stopped, still holding out his hand…toward an empty doorway.

Slowly he lowered his arm and let it dangle at his side. After a minute, I helped him to his feet and escorted him to his car.

A Brief Debrief

Does God want us to have abundant material wealth? Perhaps, for the few who can steward it safely for His purposes. But I've come to the conclusion that financial prosperity is not at the top of God's agenda for us. Here are three reasons:

- The more we focus on money and material goods, the more likely we are to succumb to greed and the love of money.

- We shouldn't be concerned about *becoming* wealthy because we're *already* extraordinarily rich. Our responsibility now is to learn what God wants us to do with that wealth, not to worry about becoming even richer.

---

* 1 Timothy 6:19

- God's spiritual blessings are worth far, far more than money or material goods. Let's pray for and seek these greater blessings.

What do you expect God to do in your life—to make you rich, or to help you use the wealth you already have to feed the hungry and to save the lost? When we go after money, we can't love people, but when we share our financial resources, we become conduits of God's love and forgiveness. And when we share God's love, God's love is also our reward.

What are the strong and biblically true aspects of the "Health and Wealth Gospel"? What are its weak and biblically false points?

Do you believe God wants to prosper you? In what way or ways?

Deeper Study

Following are several Bible passages that prosperity preachers use to support their theology. Study each passage, explain how the passage seems to support Prosperity Theology, and then explain how the passage can be misinterpreted or misused. Use other Scriptural support where appropriate, and *always* examine the context of each passage: Proverbs 3:9-10; Matthew 7:7; Mark 4:1-20; 11:24; Luke 6:38; James 4:2; Deuteronomy 28.

An Eternal Investment

I GOT THE CALL on Friday night.

I was home…alone…catching up on my vacuuming and dishes. I was about to sit down to my favourite sitcom when the phone rang. Although I knew the voice well, never had the sound of it filled me with such concern.

"Joe, it's Bill," our teacher wheezed. "Listen, could you do a favour for me?"

Suddenly TV was the last thing on my mind. "Sure, Bill. Did you call for some baking advice? I've developed some tasty dishes for the microwave."

He laughed at my attempt at humour, but his laughs turned into wracking coughs, and I waited with growing anxiety for him to recover enough to speak. Finally, he said, "I wondered if you could lead the class this Sunday. I'm not feeling too well, and I don't think I can come."

Before I could answer, he started coughing again and this time had to leave the phone for a glass of water. When he got back, he said, "Please excuse me."

"Hey, no problem," I said. "I'd be glad to fill in, although I doubt that I'll be able to rein in that unruly bunch the way you do."

"That's wonderful. Thanks. You'll do fine. If you're able, you could stop in at my place tonight or tomorrow and I'll give you my class notes and questions."

"I'll come tonight. Just give me directions."

*   *   *

Brandishing Bill's folder, I arrived at class early that Sunday. The day before, between study sessions, I had called everyone in the class to ask them to pray for Bill. And for me. Each call took only a minute or two. Well, except the call to Samantha. That ran an hour and a half.

When everyone had arrived, I could see that Max had decided not to return. Without Bill or Jennifer, the remaining group of six felt rather sparse.

"Now, guys…" I raised my hands in surrender. "I don't know these passages half as well as Bill. So go easy on me!" I received several sympathetic grins. "Samantha, would you pray for us?"

Samantha nodded and prayed what I must say, in my humble but accurate opinion, was one of the sweetest, most sincere prayers I'd ever heard.

When she finished, I thanked her, then asked, "Sue, would you read today's Scripture for us? Twice, as always, if you would."

Mrs. Coyne agreed, and we all turned in our Bibles to Mark 12:41-44. She read:

> **[41]Jesus sat down opposite the place where the offerings were put and watched the crowd putting their money into the temple treasury. Many rich people threw in large amounts. [42]But a poor widow came**

and put in two very small copper coins, worth only a fraction of a penny.

[43]Calling his disciples to him, Jesus said, "I tell you the truth, this poor widow has put more into the treasury than all the others. [44]They all gave out of their wealth; but she, out of her poverty, put in everything—all she had to live on."

When she had finished the second reading, I began. "This first question might seem simple, but think about it carefully: How much did the widow give?"

"Well," said Wayman, "the easy answer is there in verse 42. She gave **'two very small copper coins, worth only a fraction of a penny.'** But Jesus put it in different words. He said she gave **'everything—all she had to live on.'** A couple of pennies don't mean much to us, but the word *everything*—that means a lot!"

"There's one more way Jesus answers that question," said Cathy. "We normally think it's a good idea to stay away from comparisons when it comes to giving, but in this case, Jesus didn't. In verse 43, He said that the widow **'put more into the treasury than all the others.'**"

I summarized, "Two small coins...more than all the others...everything she had to live on. All three of those answers are correct. Each one reveals something different about the widow's gift. What she offered was extremely small to everyone else, but very significant to the widow herself and, therefore, extremely significant to the Lord."

I paused and was gratified when Steve and Cathy both started to scribble notes in the margins of their Bibles.

I continued, "Next, Bill has two questions relating to the *wisdom* of the widow's gift. First, was it wise for this dirt-poor woman to give everything she had?"

Steve pondered and then answered, "From a human standpoint, no, it's never wise to go broke, even for God. I don't know how long the widow could have lived on these two coins, but even if it's only a day, that might have been just enough to keep her alive until she received her next meagre bit of income. I have clients who are in pretty bad shape, but none of them are in danger of starving. I don't think the same could be said of a widow in first-century Palestine." He paused. "But I'm learning that godly giving doesn't always make sense, even when death is on the line."

If you saw a homeless person emptying his pockets into a Salvation Army donation box, what would you think? If a destitute single mother came to you at the beginning of the month and asked whether she should give her entire social assistance check to her church, what would you say?

"She wasn't making an investment in this life," said Samantha. "She was investing in eternity, and you can't make any wiser decision than that. Heaven is where her treasure would never rust or be stolen. It's still earning interest at this very moment, and it will all through eternity."

Samantha's face veritably glowed as she continued to share. *What a great heart!* I thought to myself. *I guess I have a thing or two to learn from her. That means I'll need to spend a lot more time with her. I wonder if she'd be interested in dinner this week? No, too soon. Just coffee or dessert. Or—*

"Um, Joe?" Mrs. Coyne brought me back to the present. "Do you have another question?" Samantha had finished speaking and everyone was watching me expectantly. I removed the stupid grin that I found, to my embarrassment, had spread across my face.

"Yes, yes, of course," I stammered. "I was just thinking about Sam. No! I mean, what Sam *said*."

Mrs. Coyne covered a smile. Samantha blushed. The other three politely studied their Bibles.

"Well then! Let's see...," I shuffled through Bill's notes, but required an uncomfortable moment before I could make sense of them. "Okay, next question. Let me read it straight from Bill's notes here:

The widow put her money into the temple of-
fering, which the chief priests controlled.
And it was public knowledge that Jesus and
the chief priests were at odds with each
other. Jesus Himself had exposed their
greed and hypocrisy. Then, only a short time
after the widow gives her offering, the chief
priests arranged to pay Judas money for be-
traying Christ (Mark 14:10-11). In other
words, the widow was contributing to the
same pot of money that was used to pay for
Christ's betrayal, which led to His execu-
tion! So was it wise for the widow to give at
the temple, which was run by such corrupt
leaders?

Everyone pondered the question in silence.

Then Mrs. Coyne answered tentatively, "I've never considered that before. The widow put her coins into the hands of people who were wasteful and corrupt. Have I told you all I can't stand waste?" We nodded. "And greed! I won't tolerate it." She thought for a moment longer. "No...no...I don't believe I would ever do what the widow did."

Then her rigid features softened and she said, as though to herself, "But Jesus didn't criticize her. He praised her. It doesn't make sense. I couldn't..." She settled into reverie, and there she stayed for the rest of the class.

"The widow didn't have much choice." Steve resumed the discussion. "There weren't scores of different churches and ministries to choose from. The temple was where everyone gave...their one lawful place of worship. Her choices boiled down to two: Give or don't give."

*Was it wise for this woman to give away "**all she had to live on**"?*

Why didn't Jesus criticize her for giving money into the care of the hypocritical and greedy chief priests?

Wayman grunted. "Yeah, and real giving has to be something you *feel*. Those rich people could give a lot and never know the difference. But this lady, her tiny gift cost her a lot. It really hurt!" He nodded, then added, "The rich folks probably wanted everyone to see them. But you don't see this lady jumping up and down or whooping, 'Look at me!' If Jesus hadn't said anything, no one would have paid her any heed."

Thoughtfully, Cathy said, "It was her motive and the personal cost of her gift that were important to God, not whether the gift was wise in human terms. And what *is* true wisdom, but to honour God?"

"Excellent thought, Cathy. What were the widow's motives, then?" I asked. "Why did she do this?"

We all examined the passage. Then Samantha answered, "The Bible doesn't say. But her motives must have been good, or Jesus wouldn't have praised her."

"We could guess," suggested Steve. "She may have been paying a tithe or offering required by the Law."

I said, "If Max were here, he might say that the widow planted these two coins like two seeds, expecting to reap an incredible harvest from God. You never know."

Wayman said, "Maybe she felt called by God. Or maybe Jesus even talked to her and told her to give."

"In any case," said Samantha, "I think the widow trusted in God. She was completely poor and had no other hope, so she must have learned, a long time before, to find joy in trusting God. She was so joyful she just couldn't help but give." Samantha paused and looked down. "I've had lots of people tell me not to depend on anyone, that I should get back on my own two feet." She looked back up and smiled. "But that's not the way it is with God and us.

God wants us to be totally dependent on Him, and this widow was."

We absorbed that thought for a moment. Then I said, "Bill has a homework question here, but we have some time left, so let's

Why did the poor widow give this money?

talk about it now. Verse 44 says all the others '**gave out of their wealth; but she, out of her poverty, put in everything—all she had to live on.**' The word *but* is significant, because it indicates a contrast between opposites. On the one side of the *but* were the rich people, giving out of their plenty. On the other side was this lonely widow, with nothing but two tiny coins. Her gift was worth more than all the other gifts."

Several heads nodded, so I continued, "There are only two sides to this *but*. Jesus didn't mention any in-between people. There was no middle ground. So the question is, Which side of the *but* are you on?"

At that precise moment, the classroom door opened slowly, and Reverend Moss appeared. He took two measured steps into the room and said, "I'm sorry to disturb you, but I just received some news that I expect this group would want to know. This morning Bill took a turn for the worse and was rushed to the hospital. He's in a coma, and they don't expect him to make it."

No one breathed. I glanced at Samantha; her eyes were closed.

Beside Sam, her grandmother sat, ashen-faced. Abruptly, more swiftly than I'd ever seen her move before, Mrs. Coyne rose to her feet and, without a backward look, strode from the room.

*   *   *

Bill died four days later. The various members of the group visited Bill at the hospital and prayed with him as he lay, unresponsive. I went twice with Samantha and her grand-

149

YOUR MONEY OR YOUR LIFE

mother. On her own, Mrs. Coyne went to the hospital every day, sometimes twice a day.

The following week, Reverend Moss officiated at Bill's funeral at the church. I picked up Samantha and Mrs. Coyne, and when we arrived, we were surprised to find an overwhelming throng of people. We made our way through the crowd to the sanctuary doors, where Jennifer was handing out memorial folders and directing ushers. She refused to make eye contact with any of us. Her face looked gaunt and haunted.

Eventually, we found three seats together near the back of the balcony. By the time the service started, there was standing room only.

We sang several hymns about the glory and majesty of God, and about His love and grace for us. One of the hymns, "Be Thou My Vision," began:

> Be thou my vision, O Lord of my heart;
> Naught be all else to me save that thou art.

When we reached the third verse, I couldn't help thinking of Bill's fervent trust in God and his attitude towards wealth and generosity:

> Riches I heed not, nor man's empty praise
> Thou mine inheritance, now and always;
> Thou and thou only, first in my heart,
> High King of heaven my treasure thou art.

After the hymns, Reverend Moss announced, "I'd now like to introduce to you Bill's older son, Mark. He'll deliver the eulogy for us."

Mark Smith looked to be in his late forties. He wore a black suit and had brown hair sprinkled with gray. He said, "My family and I would like to thank Reverend Moss and this church for organizing this service and for providing a great place of worship for my father, especially after we lost my mother. Dad found a family and a home here.

"Henry David Thoreau said that many people, when they come to die, discover that they have not lived. My father was not such a person. He lived life to the full.

"My grandfather on my dad's side ran a bakery for forty years, and as a young man, my father rebelled against the idea of taking over the family business. Dad went to college for a couple of years, but never graduated. Then he married my mom after dating her for just three months. Over the next two decades, he tried all sorts of business ventures and jobs. He sold kitchenware and insurance. He managed a restaurant for a while. Dad and Mom were resident managers of a huge apartment complex when I was in grade school.

"Finally, when my dad was forty-two, my grandfather had to give up running his bakery; he was too old to keep up the pace. After a fierce shouting match between them, Dad took it over. 'But I'm gonna run it my way,' I remember him declaring. Within two years, he'd opened another bakery in a nearby town, and then he kept on expanding. Many of you may not know this, because he didn't like to tell people, but my dad founded and owned the BakeFresh bakery chain."

BakeFresh! Bill never told us *that*. There were BakeFresh shops everywhere! I looked at Samantha in amazement.

Mark went on, "But the pivotal point in my father's life came when he was fifty-five, twenty years ago. Dad gave his life to Jesus Christ. My family had gone to church when I was growing up. Not every single week, but most of the time. But it was just a routine for Dad. God wasn't in charge of his life. Everything changed for him when he became a Christian.

"One major way that his life changed was financially. My father stopped expanding BakeFresh because he said it was taking too much time away from his family. The most incredible thing he did, however, was five years after becoming a Christian—he sold BakeFresh and gave away

151

almost all of the proceeds. I know this because I'm an accountant, and I handled my dad's taxes the last fifteen years. Some of you here may have benefited from his generosity.

"A couple of Dad's close friends found out about this and admonished him. 'What are you going to live on, Bill? Why not take life easy for a while?' they asked. 'That money's yours, Bill. Don't waste it.'

"Dad just said, 'Thanks to God, there's more than enough.' In fact, that became his motto: 'Thanks to God, there's more than enough.' It used to irritate me as a teenager when I would ask for a new video game or a stereo, and he'd come back with those words. But I must say that we always had lots of fun things. Dad was very generous around Christmas and birthdays. He loved to see our faces light up.

"I'd like to quote Dad's favourite Bible passage, Matthew 6:19-21:

> [19]Do not store up for yourselves treasures on earth, where moth and rust destroy, and where thieves break in and steal. [20]But store up for yourselves treasures in heaven, where moth and rust do not destroy, and where thieves do not break in and steal. [21]For where your treasure is, there your heart will be also.

"Despite his acute business sense and his enormous fortune, William Smith didn't store up any fortunes on earth. His heart was and is with God because he stored up his treasure in heaven. I know that right now he's enjoying the proceeds with God. Thank you."

*   *   *

At the reception, we met Mike Smith, the younger of Bill's two sons. We explained our relationship with Bill, in response to which Mike asked, "Oh, was it you who provided the flowers?"

"What do you mean?" Samantha asked.

"The funeral home told us that someone from the church—someone who knew Dad through a Bible study group—paid for all the flowers for the funeral. They went all out on them, and it must have cost quite a bit." I glanced at Samantha and looked around at the lavish floral display in the sanctuary. "Anyway, my family and I are very appreciative, and we wanted to thank the person personally."

> *If Jesus Christ were your banker and personal accountant, what would He say about your giving and sharing?*

"The flowers do look wonderful, but I can't take responsibility for them." Samantha turned to me. "Joe?"

"Wasn't me," I answered. "It must have been someone else."

That's when I noticed that Mrs. Coyne, who had been standing right beside Samantha, had made herself conspicuously scarce. I scanned the room and found her closely examining a pictorial display of Bill's life—a display that the three of us had perused thoroughly only minutes earlier.

Nodding slowly, I said, "But I might have a hunch."

Samantha saw the direction of my gaze, and her eyes widened with the dawning of awareness. "Hmmm. We'll have to get back to you, Mike."

Mike thanked us for coming, and we moved on.

"It all makes sense now. Grandma has been acting strange lately," Samantha said to me, quietly. "The other day she asked me to take her to the McLaren Funeral Home, but she insisted I wait out in the car for her. She *claimed* to be scouting out possible funeral arrangements for herself, and she said such things were private. But she was making arrangements for the flowers."

"Those things get expensive," I remarked. "Would she have enough for that?"

"I don't think so. I know she doesn't have any savings. She barely gets through each month on her pension. That's all she has to live on."

"How's she going to make it to next month?"

Concern showed on Samantha's face. Then she smiled and squeezed my hand. "I guess Jesus' widow was okay in the end, so I wouldn't worry about this one. Maybe I'll pay a visit to her fridge now and then, though."

I started to glance around the room when suddenly someone crashed into me from behind, nearly knocking me off my feet. Before I could even turn around, I heard an angry shout: "Hey, watch where you're going!" I looked up and saw a gruff red face...a good twelve inches higher than my own. It was Brian, the famous sermon disrupter.

"Hello to you, too, Brian," I said, rubbing my bruised shoulder.

Brian started to retort, but then softened and said, "I, uh...I guess that was my fault, huh?"

"Well, I was standing still..."

"Sorry, Joe." He stuck his huge hands into his pockets and started to walk away.

"Brian," I called after him, "did you know Bill?"

Brian stopped in his tracks. Then an amazing thing happened. He turned and, with utter humility on his face, he said, "Bill changed my life. Or I should say, God used Bill to change my life."

I couldn't help myself. "I've noticed you haven't made any loud public appearances lately."

He rolled his eyes. "I'll never live that down. You know, that very week I disrupted the sermon, my wife and I were in a car accident. My wife was injured, though thankfully it didn't turn out to be serious. My vehicle insurance had expired two days before. I hadn't renewed the insurance because I didn't have a job or any money. What a mistake that was, because I certainly didn't have eight thousand dollars to pay the other driver!

"I have no idea how Bill found out, but he showed up at the hospital the day after the accident. I was there visiting my wife and Bill prayed for us. Then, as he was leaving, he said, 'Oh, by the way, don't worry about the cost of the car accident. It's taken care of. Just don't drive uninsured again, okay, Brian?' To my wife, he said, 'And you ma'am, you get well soon! We'll be praying for you.' Then he dropped by our house the next week to see if we needed anything. He even paid for my bus pass for a month, until I found a job with benefits."

He shuffled his feet. "Nobody's every loved me that way. Now…well, now I see everything differently."

"Amazing, Brian!" I glanced at Samantha, listening beside me. "Thank you so much for telling me about that. Bill has had a profound impact on us too."

He glanced toward the exit door. "Well, I gotta go." He started to turn, then said to me, "And you watch where you're going, okay?" and gave me a sheepish grin and a wink.

I was about to comment to Samantha when I caught sight of Wayman talking with Mark Smith, so we made our way over to offer our condolences. As we approached, Wayman waved and introduced us to Mark.

Mark shook our hands, and I said, "We were in your father's Bible study on joyful generosity here at the church. We really enjoyed the class, and we admired how he led it." Wayman nodded in agreement.

Mark suddenly looked off into space, then started to smile. "Ah, yes. So *you're* Samantha." He turned to face Sam. "I have some very encouraging news for you. Before he fell sick, Dad instructed me to set up a substantial education fund for your son. Wherever he wants to go to college, he should be amply supplied." Samantha gasped. "All the paperwork is set up, waiting for Dad's signatures. But as his executor, I'll be the one signing for him."

I was stunned, but Samantha looked as though she might pass out. "I—I—can't believe…" she stammered.

"Dad wanted to wait to tell you, until after the class had finished. He would have felt embarrassed having to sit there with you every Sunday, knowing that you knew."

Beside me, Wayman cleared his throat. "Uh, I guess this is a good time to let you know, Samantha…" The widest grin I had ever seen on Wayman spread over his face. "The way Bill got me into the class in the first place was to buy the nicest car on my lot. He asked me to hold onto it for him, until he decided what to do with it." Wayman paused. Sam started to cry. "That's right. He told me two weeks ago that he wanted you to have it."

I put my arm around the joyfully distraught young lady. Mark reached out and patted her arm. Wayman shuffled his feet, didn't know what to do with his hands, and glanced around the room.

Finally, Samantha was able to speak. "Thank you both for such wonderful news. I— I don't know what else to say." She shook her head helplessly.

"I have a question that you might be able to answer, Mark," I said. "In our Bible study, your father told a few stories about a friend of his named Ron. A real estate agent? I guess Ron had…well…" I lowered my voice. "Had an affair a long time ago…kind of a heavy drinker… I wonder if you know what became of Ron? I got the feeling they were closest of friends."

Mark suddenly sobered. "They couldn't have been any closer. They were the same person. Ron is my dad's middle name…William Ronald Smith."

Samantha and I looked open-mouthed at each other. Bill had been even more a product of God's amazing grace than we had thought.

I suddenly realized we had been dominating Mark's attention, and several other people were waiting to talk with him. "Thank you for enlightening us," I said. We each shook his hand, and then we started to walk away. But I turned back. "God bless you."

Mark smiled and nodded. "He already has, my friend. God has blessed me all my years and for all eternity by giving me a father like my dad."

A Brief Debrief

I have to say that was one of the most powerful weeks of my life. One central truth stands out in my mind as I look back, and it serves also to summarize the entire study series. It's this: *The impact of our godly giving doesn't end with the end of this life; it continues on in our own eternal life, and in the eternal lives of others...forever.*

Because Bill gave...and gave...and gave...hundreds, maybe thousands, of people will enjoy God for eternity— and enjoy Him more deeply than if Bill had followed the world's wisdom with his wealth. The best way I can say thanks to my teacher is to follow his example with all of my heart.

So...thanks, Bill.

Most of all, thank You, Lord. You're the most lavish Giver of all.

Compare the poor widow with the rich young ruler in Luke 18:18-30. Why was she willing to give everything, while he was not?

Compare this poor widow with Zacchaeus in Luke 19:1-10. How are they similar? How are they different?

The Bible tells us repeatedly to give to the poor and to take care of the lost and oppressed. And yet here was a destitute woman giving all she had. What can we learn from this passage?

ON THE ONE-YEAR ANNIVERSARY of Bill's death, I took Samantha, her son, Cody, and her grandmother to the cemetery where Bill was buried. Mrs. Coyne wanted to pay her respects with a bouquet of flowers.

It was a warm spring day, but the aged trees that stood watch over the cemetery kept us shaded and cool. Standing beside Bill's grave, I held Samantha's hand and enjoyed the feel of the engagement ring I'd given her one month earlier. We planned a late summer wedding.

"Look at the epitaph," Samantha said, gesturing at the gravestone. Under "William Ronald Smith" and the dates of his birth and death, the inscription read:

HE SENT IT ON AHEAD

MATTHEW 6:19-21

REVELATION 3:17-20

I nodded and smiled. "Bill did send his treasure on ahead, like Matthew 6 tells us. It's all safe in heaven." I searched my memory. "But what does the Revelation passage say?"

Samantha pulled a pocket-sized New Testament out of her purse and turned to the back. She read aloud:

> [17]You say, 'I am rich; I have acquired wealth and do not need a thing.' But you do not realize that you are wretched, pitiful, poor, blind and naked. [18]I counsel you to buy from me gold refined in the fire, so you can become rich; and white clothes to wear, so you can cover your shameful nakedness; and salve to put on your eyes, so you can see. [19]Those whom I love I rebuke and discipline. So be earnest, and repent. [20]Here I am! I stand at the door and knock. If anyone hears my voice and opens the door, I will come in and eat with him, and he with me.

I laughed, but not because the thought was happy. "Bill definitely heard Christ knocking and he responded big-time. But so many of us don't respond. We say we don't need a thing, but we're actually wretched, pitiful, naked. No wonder we don't hear Christ knocking on our door—we have the stereo or TV cranked up too loud. Or maybe we're down in the garage, lost in admiration for our car or some other toy."

"Or we don't hear His knock because we're away from home, out slaving for money to maintain the lifestyle," Samantha said.

"The love of money is deafening," said Mrs. Coyne.

We were quiet for a moment. Then Sam said, "Joyful Generosity—I learned a lot from that class."

"So did I," Mrs. Coyne said. "It changed my life. And for an old bat like me, that's amazing!"

"It's amazing at any age," I responded.

After a few more minutes, we walked back to the car.

*　　*　　*

In the years since then, I've tried to keep up with everyone from the class.

In addition to Cody, whom I love as my own son, Samantha and I now have two daughters—Susan and Cathy. Our commitment to joyful generosity has been sorely challenged several times, but on each occasion, one of us has reminded the other of the numerous miracles of God's faithfulness we've seen, and we've managed to stay the course.

Sam's grandmother is still very much alive. We drop by her apartment at least once or twice a week. (I'd never want to miss my required weekly allowance of ranting about wasteful spending.) Actually, if anyone can be accused of being "wasteful," it's Sue Coyne. Sam and I are becoming prematurely gray with anxiety over some of Sue's lavish gifts to ministry and to needy people. But she has never missed a meal, she's never paid her rent late, and there's always enough to cover her monthly medications.

Wayman's business is thriving—mainly because he has gained a reputation as the most honest dealer in town. He and I still meet once a month for financial accountability. There was that period of two months when he kept cancelling our appointments. He'd had a bad business year, and…well, let's just say old habits die hard. But in the long run, Wayman has sustained his faith in God to provide for him at least as generously as Wayman gives to others.

Jennifer, on the other hand, has remained as consistent as ever. She still works for the church, making sure everyone abides by the rules. She still gives exactly ten percent of every paycheque—no more, no less. (She mentions it to at least two or three people a month.) Three years ago, she married a young bank vice-president. They don't plan to have kids. Family would interfere with their lifestyle.

Cathy and Bob have never completely shaken their nervousness about providing for their family—especially after the baby was born. Another mouth to feed. They make occasional forays into the land of joyous generosity, which is better than they were doing before. But, as I've already said, old habits die hard.

Steve retired a year ago, but not before Sam and I retained him for a few years as our financial consultant. His counselling strategy has shifted significantly—at least when it comes to Christian clients. He still pays attention to common sense and conventional wisdom, but not nearly as much as he used to.

Last time I heard any word of Max, he had moved across the country in pursuit of some wild financial venture he felt God calling him to. I have no idea whether his seeds have flourished into prosperity or not.

And Bill, of course, is not only thoroughly enjoying all the treasure he stored away in heaven, but he is spending eternity with the greatest Treasure of all…the God who loves. And loves to give.

SUPPLEMENTAL STUDIES

The Parable of the Talents: A Time-Sensitive Investment

Read twice—*Matthew 24:1-3 and 25:14-30.*

FYI: Matthew 24-25 is a single teaching unit, known as the Olivet Discourse. The word "it" at the very beginning of the Parable of the Talents refers to the kingdom of heaven (see 25:1).

FYI: The word "talent" in this passage comes from the Greek word *talanton*, which refers to a monetary unit of great value. Many people misinterpret this passage, believing it to speak primarily of receiving skills and abilities from God and using them for Him. We come closer to a meaningful translation of the passage if we replace the word *talent* with *valuable coin* or even a large contemporary denomination, such as *a thousand dollars.*

Since the money in the passage represents everything God has entrusted to our care, skills and abilities are indeed included, but they are only one category among many other valuable gifts from God.

Questions for Study and Application

1. Whose money was being invested in the parable?

2. Verse 15 says that the master entrusted varying amounts of money to the three servants, **"each according to his ability."** What ability do you think the master took into account? How might God evaluate your ability to manage His wealth?

3. Why did the first two servants act faithfully with what they were given? What was the motivation of the third, wicked servant?

4. What kinds of investments today are symbolized by the investments of the first two servants? (Compare with 24:45; 25:34-40.)

5. Why did Jesus paint such a vivid picture of the worthless servant's doom in verse 30? Why did He end the parable with this negative image rather than on a positive note?

6. In Matthew 24:3, the disciples asked Jesus about the end of the age. How does the Parable of the Talents answer these questions?

7. What is the central message of the Parable of the Talents?

8. If you knew that, sometime in the next five years, Jesus would return and call in His investments from you, what would you do differently with your money? Your abilities? Your time?

Deeper Study

Briefly summarize the flow of the Olivet Discourse (Matthew 24-25). How does this context help you interpret the Parable of the Talents?

Providing for and
Training My Family

Read twice—1 Timothy 5:3-8.

Questions for Study and Application

Some of the following questions apply to parents. If you do not have children, you might still answer these questions either in anticipation of your future family, or as you consider ways to encourage other families.

1. According to 1 Timothy 5:3-8, describe the ways we must care for family. In particular, what is our responsibility to elderly family members?

2. Why was Paul's warning so strong toward those who failed to care for family?

3. What are the most common reasons someone might fail to care for his or her family?

4. How does one balance responsibility to family with responsibility to give to ministry and the needy?

5. Which other Bible passages contain principles pertaining to providing materially for one's family?

6. In Luke 14:26, Jesus said, "**If anyone comes to me and does not hate his father and mother, his wife and children, his brothers and sisters—yes, even his own life—he cannot be my disciple.**" How can we reconcile this statement with 1 Timothy 5:8?

7. Read Proverbs 22:6. How are you training your children in giving, spending, saving, and the true value of material wealth? (Or how are you planning to do this?) How do you teach by your own example? By your instruction? By involving your children in your family's acts of generosity?

8. What is the danger of giving your children too much in the way of money or things? Is there danger in giving them too little? How can you find God's balance?

The Parable of the Good Samaritan: A Heavenly Investment

Read twice—Luke 10:25-37.

FYI: In verse 27, the Law expert was quoting from Deuteronomy 6:5 and Leviticus 19:18.

FYI: Jesus' Jewish listeners were probably expecting the third passer-by to be a Jewish layman. They were no doubt scandalized to hear that he was a Samaritan, considered by the Jews to be an unclean half-breed.

Questions for Study and Application

1. The Levites were the special Jewish tribe set apart for priestly duties, and the priests were the only ones who could perform the special acts of worship at the Temple. Why didn't these spiritual leaders help the beaten man?

2. What reasons do you sometimes use for not helping someone in need? In what ways are these valid? In what ways are they merely excuses for avoiding obedience?

3. The road between Jerusalem and Jericho was dangerous in those days, so many people travelled in large groups. Agree or disagree: "Many needy people have gotten themselves into their own difficult situations. Helping them too much would simply enable them." Explain your answer.

4. What risks did the Samaritan take in this story? What risks do you run as you reach out to the unlovely people in your life?

5. What types of "injuries," other than physical ones, might we encounter in people who are hurting? How should this parable guide our response to such people?

6. How might you plan ahead so that you're ready to help others when needs arise?

7. We cannot help all the poor and hurting people in this world. How can we demonstrate God's love for the poor and oppressed in light of the immensity of the need?

8. Jesus instructed, **"Go and do likewise."** How will you follow the Samaritan's example?

The Rich Man and Lazarus (Personally, I'd Rather Be Lazarus)

Read twice—Luke 16:19-31.

FYI: Many people in Jesus' audience would have been surprised that the rich man went to hell and Lazarus to heaven. Riches were often seen as a sign of God's blessing and poverty a sign of His curse. As we've seen throughout this study series, this is not necessarily true.

Questions for Study and Application

1. Why did the rich man go to hell? Why did Lazarus go to heaven?

2. We know from many Bible passages that we are saved by grace, not by works. Ephesians 2:8-10 says, "**[8]For it is by grace you have been saved, through faith—and this not from yourselves, it is the gift of God— [9]not by works, so that no one can boast. [10]For we are God's workmanship, created in Christ Jesus to do good works, which God prepared in advance for us**

to do." How can we reconcile this Ephesians passage—and all we know about God's grace—with the story of the Rich Man and Lazarus?

3. The rich man couldn't cross the chasm to Lazarus after death. Why didn't he cross the chasm that existed between himself and Lazarus *before* they died?

4. Describe the chasms that exist between you and some of the needy people around you. What can be done to cross them? What are the difficulties in crossing them?

5. Who are the sick people on your doorstep, literally or figuratively? Who are the people who long to eat what falls from your table?

6. How does this passage make you feel? If you feel guilty, is it false guilt or conviction from God?

7. What is Jesus' central message in this story? Will you do anything differently because of it?

Unacceptable Giving:
The Deadly Consequences

Read twice—Matthew 23:23-24; Genesis 4:1-8;
and Acts 4:32-5:11.

Questions for Study and Application

Matthew 23:23-24

1. Why did the Pharisees and teachers of the Law give a tenth of their spices? Why did they neglect **the more important matters of the Law**?

2. What areas of obedience do we have a tendency to focus on? What areas of obedience do we tend to neglect? What must we do in order to heed the greater (and lesser) parts of God's instruction to us?

Genesis 4:1-8

3. Why did God look with favour on Abel and his offering but not on Cain and his offering?

4. Cain's sinful attitude led to yet another sin—murder. How might sin in our attitudes toward money and possessions lead us to sin in other ways?

Acts 4:32-5:11

5. How did the early church manage to eradicate all need in their midst? Could we do this in our churches today?

6. What was Ananias and Sapphira's sin? Are you guilty of this same sin?

7. **"Great fear seized the whole church"** when they heard about the deaths of Ananias and Sapphira. Do you respond with appropriate sobriety and godly fear when you see God's judgment on sin?

General Questions

8. What similarities do you see between the Pharisees, Cain, and Ananias and Sapphira?

9. In Hosea 6:6, the Lord says, **"For I desire mercy, not sacrifice, and acknowledgement of God rather than burnt offerings."** Jesus quoted from this passage in Matthew 9:13 and 12:7. What can we learn from this teaching?

10. Does God ever redeem unacceptable gifts? How might he do this?

11. Is there anything you need to confess to God now? If so, read 1 John 1:8-10 carefully, and talk to Him.